DIVERGENCE

Examining Jewish-Christian
Relations in the Early Church

R. L. SOLBERG

WILLIAMSON
COLLEGE
PRESS

www.RLSolberg.com

ISBN: 978-1-7336721-3-9 (print)
ISBN: 978-1-7336721-4-6 (digital)

Williamson College Press
274 Mallory Station Road,
Franklin, Tennessee 37067
williamsoncc.edu | info@williamsoncc.edu

To Paul and Daniel

Two are better than one, because they have a good reward for their toil. For if they fall, one will lift up his fellow. But woe to him who is alone when he falls and has not another to lift him up!

Ecclesiastes 4:9-10

Contents

Preface

When I began the research that eventually turned into this book, I had no idea the world was about to witness another wave of anti-Semitism. It breaks my heart when any people group suffers hostility and prejudice at the hands of anyone else. I find it even more tragic when the people doing the hating are Christians, and the people being hated are Jews. Not all Christians harbor anti-Semitism, of course. But the problem is pervasive enough that I felt moved to do something about it. That is why I am donating every penny of profit from this book to a non-profit organization that fights anti-Semitism around the world. (See DivergenceBook.com for details.) And I was thrilled when my publisher Williamson College said they wanted to join me in that effort.

There is a unique, complex historical relationship between Jews and Christians. Israel is a nation supernaturally called forth by God. The historical thread that began with Abraham sometime around 1,900 BC has evolved down through the centuries into a glorious, colorful tapestry. It continues to grow today, and we Christians have been woven in.

> For in Christ Jesus you are all sons of God, through faith.
> For as many of you as were baptized into Christ have put
> on Christ. There is neither Jew nor Greek, there is neither
> slave nor free, there is no male and female, for you are all
> one in Christ Jesus. And if you are Christ's, then you are

Abraham's offspring, heirs according to promise.

(Galatians 3:26-29)

Christians can rightly view the Jewish people as our spiritual cousins. Indeed, the Gospel is a Jewish story. This is something the early Christian writers roundly affirmed.

Interestingly, anti-Semitism is not the main point of this book. My research was initially inspired by the apologetic work I do in defending biblical Christianity against the growing modern heresy known as *Torahism*. These are folks who profess faith in Jesus, and at the same time, teach that Christians are required to "keep Torah." (You may have heard of the Hebrew Roots Movement or the Black Hebrew Israelites?) These groups believe we should be keeping all of the Old Testament Laws given to Israel, including the Saturday Sabbath, dietary restrictions, biblical feasts, and so on. At the root of Torahism is the idea that Christian theology was corrupted in the early centuries of the faith by rampant anti-Semitism. It is this foundational belief that I set out to investigate.

My goal was to understand the true nature of Jewish-Christian relations through the first three centuries of the faith. I chose this specific period of history because it is here that Torahism (among others) claims Christian theology was hopelessly corrupted. The Council of Nicaea in AD 325 is seen as a crystallizing event. It was there that the Church officially embraced the anti-Jewish attitudes of the early Christians. Right?

After studying scores of early writings and the work of modern Jewish and Christian scholars, I discovered things weren't nearly as black-and-white as we think. The relationship between Jews and early Christians was complex and nuanced. As Jewish scholar Daniel Boyarin points out in the preface to his book *Borderlines*, "The affiliation between what we call Judaism and what we call Christianity is much more complex than most scholars, let alone most lay folk, imagine" (p. xi). The two groups were entwined by a shared history, common sacred texts, and a conjoined theology. They were each trying to work out what this whole Jesus thing meant. And they were fumbling for solid footing amid ever-shifting political and cultural sands.

I discovered that anti-Jewish sentiment absolutely did exist in early Christianity, but it wasn't what our modern minds would expect. The clashes were chiefly based on issues of theology, not race. In fact, racial theory in antiquity was markedly different from today, which had to be figured into my findings. In addition, during these early centuries, Jewish-Christian tensions were more of a two-street than we realize.

In the end, I was both enlightened and encouraged by my research into the formative centuries of our faith. And I pray you find a little of each in this book, as well.

For His glory,
R. L. Solberg
Nashville, TN
May 21, 2021
rls@rlsolberg.com

Introduction

There is a growing religious movement known as *Torahism*,[1] which claims the sermons preached every Sunday in Christian churches contain a long-corrupted theology. The root of this allegation is ultimately traced back to the earliest centuries of Christianity, in which it is claimed anti-Semitism ran rampant among the early Church fathers. Torahism holds that these anti-Jewish views ultimately came to a head at the Council of Nicaea in AD 325. It was there, Torahism claims, that the Christian Church officially separated itself from the Jewish roots of the faith. At Nicaea, the Church chose Easter over Passover, Sunday worship over the Saturday Sabbath, and made other declarations aimed at divesting Christianity of its Jewish heritage. Thus, says Torahism, the teachings initially given by Jesus and the Apostles had become corrupt by the time of Nicaea and remain so today. Could that be true? In this book, we will examine the first three centuries of Jewish-Christian relations. Our goal is to piece together an accurate understanding of the nature and degree of anti-Jewish sentiment present during this historical period. And, further, to see if we can determine what sort of impact anti-Jewish sentiments had on Christian theology.

Our survey will begin with the New Testament (NT) writings, focusing on passages that convey the theology and attitudes of Jesus

---

[1] *Torahism* is an umbrella term for the belief that followers of Jesus are required to keep the Law of Moses. It is also known as Torah-observant Christianity. Torahism includes groups such as *Hebrew Roots Movement*, *Black Hebrew Israelites, 119 Ministries*, and others.

and the NT authors concerning Judaism and the Jewish people. We will use the results of this analysis as our baseline. Next, using the writings of Church fathers and rabbis—supplemented with the work of modern Christian and Jewish scholars—we will trace Christian theology and its attitudes toward the Jewish people from the New Testament through the writings of the early Church fathers to the Council of Nicaea in AD 325. Finally, we will compare the state of Christian theology and attitudes at the conclusion of the Council of Nicaea to our NT baseline.

Our goal is to determine if, by the conclusion of the Council of Nicaea, Christian theology was altered due to anti-Jewish attitudes. And if so, how, and to what extent, was it changed. To help with this comparison, two contentious Jewish-Christian issues will serve as theological markers. First is the Jewish Sabbath, which is observed on the last day of the week, versus the Christian tradition of gathering on the first day of the week, Sunday, as the Lord's Day. Second is the matter of the Jewish observance of Passover versus the Christian celebration of Easter. These two issues are discussed in the New Testament, in the writings of the early Christians, and at Nicaea. As we work our way through the first three centuries of Jewish-Christian relations, these two issues will provide us with a consistent point of measurement of the degree and nature of anti-Jewish impact on Christian theology.

CHAPTER 1

Historical Context

BECAUSE OUR STUDY CENTERS ON EARLY WRITINGS AND EVENTS, it's important we begin by establishing a framework for the historical era we're examining. This will give us the proper context for the ancient documents we're going to review. Let's take a brief look at three areas: persecution, public discourse, and racial relations.

PERSECUTION

The legal status of Judaism and Christianity differed within the Roman Empire during the ante-Nicene era (~AD 30-325). Judaism was considered a *religio licita* (permitted religion) and, as such, was largely exempt from the requirements the Romans imposed on other religions. However, Jews did undergo occasional persecution at the hands of Rome. For example, in AD 19, Tiberius expelled the Jews from Rome,[1] and thirty years later, in AD 49, Claudius did the same.[2] Rome originally saw Christianity as just another Jewish sect. That is until AD 64 when the emperor Nero blamed a massive fire on the "the Christians." After that, Christianity was viewed as separate from Judaism and branded a *religio illicita* (illegal religion).

---

[1] Suetonius, *The Lives of the Twelve Caesars: To Which Are Added, His Lives of the Grammarians, Rhetoricians, and Poets*, trans. Alexander Thomson (Charleston, South Carolina: Bibliobazaar, 2008), 36.
[2] Ibid., Claudius 25.4

The bourgeoning Christian church suffered a great deal of persecution at the hands of the Roman state. But maltreatment also came from some groups who held opposing beliefs, such as Jews and Gnostics. Martyrdom was not an uncommon occurrence. Some Christians, such as Ignatius, counted themselves blessed to be martyred for their faith. After being called to Rome to face execution, Ignatius wrote the Roman church, begging them not to interfere with his impending death: "Pray leave me to be a meal for the beasts, for it is they who can provide my way to God. I am His wheat, ground fine by the lion's teeth to be made purest bread for Christ."[3] And, indeed, that is the fate Ignatius met.

Christian persecution ebbed and flowed across the Roman Empire, differing from region to region. In extreme cases, believers were beheaded, crucified, burned at the stake, used as torches to light roads, fed to wild beasts in the arena, and met other violent ends for their profession of faith in Jesus. Roman authorities frequently forced suspected Christians to pay homage to the emperor as a deity to test their faith. (Jews were exempted from this obligation as long as they paid the *Fiscus Judaicus.*) There are recorded occasions when Christians of Jewish descent would claim to be Jewish and were taken to the local synagogue to validate their declaration. Jewish authorities were apt to refuse to acknowledge the Christian as a fellow Jew, which sometimes led to their execution.[4]

Because Jewish religious leaders wielded a level of authority and political clout in Jerusalem, they could bring a great deal of pressure on the developing Christian community. As we will look at in detail in the next section, the New Testament records much of the persecution that early Christians endured at the hands of Jewish religious

---

[3] Ignatius, *Epistle to the Romans* (AD 110).
[4] Robin Lane Fox, *Pagans, and Christians in the Mediterranean World: From the Second Century AD to the Conversion of Constantine* (London: Penguin, 2006).

authorities. Writings after the New Testament reveal that Jewish leadership continued to persecute Christians even after the fall of Jerusalem in AD 70. Jewish Christians were increasingly pushed out of the synagogue and lost the protected status granted to Judaism. While Christians during the ante-Nicene era spoke out against unbelieving Jews, they stopped short of maltreatment or violence.[5]

PUBLIC DISCOURSE & RELIGIOUS CONVICTIONS

In the Roman Empire, the nature of public discourse and the intensity of religious convictions were markedly different from today. Thus, to accurately evaluate literature from this period, it is crucial to understand the culture and climate in which those writings emerged. What seems shocking to our modern Western minds (such as burning someone at the stake for their religious beliefs) was the reality in which the early Christian writers, including the New Testament authors, operated. In antiquity, one's religious convictions could be a matter of life and death.

In a culture where both state and religious authorities would oppress and even execute people based on matters of faith, the nature and intensity of public discourse naturally followed suit. Believe it or not, modern dialogue in the public sphere is significantly more civil and respectful than the exchanges of the Roman Empire during this era. Scholars Smith and Covino note "praise and blame in the form of panegyric [elaborate praise] and invective [insulting or abusive language] were essential components of Greek culture"[6] and "much of Roman rhetoric and literature, including poetry, is encomiastic

---

[5] Sadly, Christianity did not remain so. Beginning late in the fourth century, parts of Christendom took a decidedly unbiblical turn in their opinions and treatment of the Jewish people. Christian leaders such as John Chrysostom began preaching against the Jews as a people, using disparaging and hateful rhetoric. Over the centuries, this grew into the Christian anti-Semitism we see today.
[6] Christopher Smith and Ralph Covino, *Praise and Blame in Roman Republican Rhetoric* (Swansea: Classical Press of Wales, 2011), p. 3.

[praising highly] or vituperative [bitter and abusive] in form."[7] It was not uncommon for public conversations between opponents to include caustic comments of scorn and ridicule that would cause our modern sensibilities to bristle. Ancient historian Dr. Martin Jehne of Technische Universität Dresden offers an example:

> The famous speaker and politician Marcus Tullius Cicero (106-43 BC), for instance, when he defended his supporter Sestius, did not shrink from publicly accusing the enemy Clodius of incest with brothers and sisters.

Even in ancient Rome, incest was an unlawful sexual practice and considered deeply immoral.[8]

RACIAL RELATIONS IN ANTIQUITY

It is also important to establish an understanding of racial relations in antiquity. We hear heartbreaking modern-day stories of anti-Semitic Christians verbally and physically attacking Jews as "Christ-killers." Scenes like this play out between school kids and grown adults alike. It is a pernicious thread of sin that has wound its way down the centuries. In the 16th century, Martin Luther, the father of the Reformation, called for the destruction of Jews in Germany, writing, "First, set fire to their synagogues . . . Second, I advise that their houses also be razed and destroyed."[9] In the documentary film *Forbidden Peace*, Rose Price, a Polish Jew and Holocaust survivor, recounts how the Nazi camp guards would tell her they were following Jesus' orders as they struck her.[10] (Amazingly, Rose later came to faith in Christ.)

---

[7] Ibid., p. 8.

[8] Mihai Andrei, "In Ancient Rome, Political Discourse Was Sometimes Like an Internet Fight," ZME Science, August 24, 2018, www.zmescience.com/science/history-science/rome-political-discourse-insults-24082018/.

[9] Martin Luther, *On the Jews & Their Lies*. (Gottfried & Fritz, Trans.) eBook, Part IV Para. 2.

[10] *Forbidden Peace*, directed by Beth Freeman Kenison (Jews for Jesus, 2004).

Many historians believe that the foundation of the worst atrocity the Jewish people ever endured—the Holocaust—was fomented during the 1,500 years of anti-Jewish sentiment that preceded it. Sadly, there is no denying the existence of anti-Semitism. And as we'll see in the coming chapters, this sort of hatred and persecution of the Jewish people is unbiblical. It is contrary to the teachings of Jesus and the New Testament authors.

However, to apply the modern concept of "racism" to ancient cultures—in particular, the Christian view of Jews—is an anachronistic error. The economic and social tensions that shape the modern understanding of anti-Semitism were not present in the ancient Near East. Jewish scholar Shaye Cohen explains:

> Anti-Semitism did not exist in antiquity. This term was coined in 1879 by a German writer who wished to bestow "scientific" respectability on the hatred of Jews by arguing that Jews and Germans belong to different species of humanity ("races"). But the ancients did not have anything resembling a racial theory . . . They observed that different nations had different moral characteristics . . . But did not explain these differences by appeal to what we would call a racial theory. Instead, they argued that climate, soil, and water determined both the physical and moral characteristics of nations. Therefore, the notion of anti-Semitism is inappropriate to antiquity.[11]

While anti-Semitism as a racial issue did not exist in antiquity, anti-Jewish sentiment certainly did. The anti-Jewishness of the non-Christian world was chiefly political rather than racial or religious. Cohen notes,

---

[11] Shaye J. D. Cohen, *From the Maccabees to the Mishnah* (Louisville, KY: Westminster John Knox Press, 2014), p. 39.

7

The persecution of Jews by Epiphanes, the attack on Alexandrian Jewry by the mob, and the destruction of the temple by Titus were each caused by local factors and not by some deep-rooted "anti-Judaism." Nevertheless, the literary propaganda spawned by these conflicts helped shape the "anti-Semitic" image of the Jew of later generations.[12]

What, then, is to be made of the "racial tension" found in the New Testament between Jews and Samaritans? This, too, is an anachronism of the modern racial mindset. The animosity between Jews and Samaritans did not emerge as an issue of race but of theology. The Samaritans traced their lineage to the time of Eli. They considered themselves of Jewish ethnicity, descending through the Israelite tribes of Ephraim and Manasseh.[13] The difference is that the Samaritans followed the Israelite Samaritan Version of the Torah and believed theirs was the true and proper faith held by the ancient Israelites. They considered Judaism a corrupted religion brought back by the Jewish exiles returning from Babylon. A principal difference was that Samaritans believed God was to be worshiped at Shechem (Mount Gerizim) rather than Jerusalem.[14] Therefore, at the risk of oversimplification, we might compare the hostility between Jews and Samaritans to that of the Hatfields and the McCoys—a feud based on historical grievances rather than racial differences.

Similarly, while anti-Jewish sentiment existed in the early Church, it was not an issue of ethnicity but rather a clash of religious convictions. And the conflict went both ways. Christians argued vehemently against unbelieving Jews on the basis that Judaism denied

---

[12] Ibid., p. 41.

[13] B. C. Babcock et al., eds., *The Lexham Bible Dictionary* (Bellingham, WA: Lexham Press, 2016), Samaritans.

[14] Lisbeth S Fried, *Ezra and the Law in History and Tradition* (Columbia, South Carolina: University Of South Carolina, 2014), p. 198. (See John 4:19.)

Jesus. Jews argued vigorously against the Christians because they were breaking with centuries of Jewish tradition and teaching heresy.

As this book unfolds and we dig into some of the early Christian writings—including those of the New Testament authors—the reader is encouraged to enter into the mind frame of the ancient Near East. If we hope to accurately understand the nature of the relationship between Jews and Christians in the first few centuries after Christ, we need to divest ourselves of our modern Western notions of issues like racial theory, freedom of religion, and the separation of church and state.

CHAPTER 2

New Testament Writings

A COMPLETE AND EXHAUSTIVE SURVEY of the New Testament writings on this issue is well beyond the scope of this book. But we can build an accurate picture by focusing on the passages that contain the most direct and explicit teachings regarding Judaism and the Jewish people.

The writings of the New Testament are dated between roughly AD 50-100. The earliest books are believed to have been written within thirty years of the Crucifixion.[1] This puts them well within the lifetimes of those who knew and followed Jesus and those who witnessed the events recorded by the New Testament writers. Conservative scholars believe that the overwhelming majority of the New Testament writings were completed before the destruction of Jerusalem in AD 70. In other words, these writings arose early in Christianity. And they were circulated widely. Moreover, with the possible exception of Luke, the New Testament writers were all Jewish. Indeed, Jewish scholars Landman and Cohen tell us:

> Most of the writers of the various parts were Jews, and the writings were designed for Jewish readers who had embraced the Christian faith. The authors drew more or

---

[1] While we cannot date these ancient writings with absolute confidence, the following books are generally accepted to have been written before AD 60: Romans, 1 and 2 Thessalonians, Philippians, Galatians, 1 and 2 Corinthians.

less from contemporary Jewish ideas, ethics, legends, parables, and sayings.[2]

We know that the modern concepts of racism and racial theory were foreign to the minds of the ancients. And there is further evidence that the conflicts documented in the New Testament are not properly viewed as racial issues. Jesus and His earliest followers were all Jewish, and so were their persecutors. These disputes were not fueled by anti-Semitism but, as we will see, by theological differences. The New Testament offers a remarkably clear view of the nature of early Jewish-Christian relations, a view that predates even the label of "Christians." From the book of Acts, we know that early Christian preaching began in the Jewish synagogues of the diaspora and amassed a following from both Jews and Gentiles. Jesus, the apostles, and the early Christian church relied on the Hebrew Scriptures as its Bible. As historian Everett Ferguson points out, Judaism provided the religious context for the early Christian church.[3]

By concentrating on the teachings of two Jewish men—the apostle Paul and Jesus Himself—we can develop a well-rounded perspective on the New Testament's teachings about how Christians are to regard Judaism and the Jewish people.

THE APOSTLE PAUL

The apostle Paul is uniquely qualified to give us a biblical perspective on this issue. When we first meet him in the pages of Scripture, he is a proudly Jewish man who considers himself a "Hebrew of Hebrews" (Phil 3:5). He was on a mission to wipe out this new Jewish sect that

---

[2] Isaac Landman and Simon Cohen, *The Universal Jewish Encyclopedia: The Seven-Branched Light; a Reading Guide and Index to the Universal Jewish Encyclopedia.* (New York, Ktav Pub. House, 1969), p. 174.
[3] Everett Ferguson, *Church History: The Rise and Growth of the Church in Its Cultural, Intellectual, and Political Context,* Vol. 1 (Grand Rapids: Zondervan, 2013), p. 31.

would not stop teaching and preaching about *Yeshua HaMashiach* (Jesus the Messiah). Of his time as a Jewish persecutor of Christians, he wrote:

> For you have heard of my former life in Judaism, how I persecuted the church of God violently and tried to destroy it. And I was advancing in Judaism beyond many of my own age among my people, so extremely zealous was I for the traditions of my fathers. (Galatians 1:13–14, ESV)

Luke reports that Paul ravaged the church, and "entering house after house, he dragged off men and women and committed them to prison" (Acts 8:3). Moreover,

> breathing threats and murder against the disciples of the Lord, [Paul] went to the high priest and asked him for letters to the synagogues at Damascus, so that if he found any belonging to the Way, men or women, he might bring them bound to Jerusalem. (Acts 9:1-2)[4]

As a Jew, Paul was so convinced he should oppose these new Nazarenes that he imprisoned many of them and even cast his vote to put some to death. He confesses he "punished them often in all the synagogues and tried to make them blaspheme, and in raging fury against them I persecuted them even to foreign cities" (Acts 26:9-11).

And then Paul met the risen Jesus on the road to Damascus (Acts 9:1-19). Following this supernatural experience, he became a fervent follower of Christ. Paul was converted to "the Way," the same Jewish sect he had been persecuting. Scholars typically date Paul's conversion to AD 34–37,[5] which means his persecution of the early Christians may have even begun during Jesus' earthly ministry. Moreover, Paul's

---

[4] See also: Acts 22:4-5; 1 Corinthians 15:9; Galatians 1:13, 23; Philippians 3:6.
[5] Paul Barnett, *Jesus & the Rise of Early Christianity: A History of New Testament Times* (Downers Grove, IL: Intervarsity Press, 1999), p. 21.

conversion is dated to as little as a year after the Resurrection, perhaps occurring within months of his attendance at (and approval of) the execution of Christianity's first-known martyr, Stephen (Acts 7:54-8:1, 22:20). Noted Jewish scholar Alan Segal admits:

> However much I may disagree with Paul, my reading accedes to the authenticity of Paul's conversion experience. Paul considered himself part of a new Jewish sect and hoped to convince both fellow Christians and Jews of his vision of redemption.[6]

Paul had transformed from a Jew zealously persecuting Christians to a Christian being persecuted by Jews. And God used him to write nearly one-third of the New Testament. Who better to provide us with a biblical perspective on this issue? And we don't want to miss this crucial fact: Paul's conversion to Christianity did not require him to leave his Jewishness behind. On the contrary, he continued to celebrate his Hebrew heritage, even after his conversion. As a Christian, Paul wrote to his fellow Jews:

> If anyone else thinks he has reason for confidence in the flesh, I have more: circumcised on the eighth day, of the people of Israel, of the tribe of Benjamin, a Hebrew of Hebrews; as to the law, a Pharisee; as to zeal, a persecutor of the church; as to righteousness under the law, blameless. (Philippians 3:4b-6)

And during his arrest at the temple in Jerusalem, Paul began his speech to the unruly crowd with a declaration of his Jewish bona fides:

---

[6] Alan F Segal, *Paul the Convert: The Apostolate and Apostasy of Saul the Pharisee* (New Haven: Yale University Press, 1992), p. xiv.

I am a Jew, born in Tarsus in Cilicia, but brought up in this city, educated at the feet of Gamaliel[7] according to the strict manner of the law of our fathers, being zealous for God as all of you are this day. (Acts 22:3)

Paul's Letter to the Romans

In Romans 9-11, Paul provides one of the New Testament's most comprehensive teachings regarding the relationship between Jews and Christians. These three chapters specifically address the unique role of the Jews in God's redemptive story and the relationship between Jews and Gentiles. We will use this text as our foundation as we begin to establish a biblical perspective on how Christians ought to regard Judaism and the Jewish people.

The opening verses of each of these three chapters give us a glimpse into Paul's heart on this issue. As a Christian, Paul writes of the "great sorrow and anguish" (9:2) he feels for his fellow Jews, of his "desire and prayer" for their salvation (10:1), and of his confidence that God has not rejected them (11:1). In fact, he expresses such deep love for his fellow Jews he would be willing to give up his own salvation if they could all be saved: "For I could wish that I myself were accursed and cut off from Christ for the sake of my brothers, my kinsmen according to the flesh" (Rom 9:3).[8] Paul's sorrow over Israel's unbelief is even more heart-rending to him because of her unique privileges. Paul lists eight specific blessings given by God to Israel:

---

[7] Gamaliel was a chief elder in the Sanhedrin and the grandson of famed Jewish sage Hillel. According to the Jewish Mishnah, Gamaliel was one of the greatest teachers in all of Judaism: "Since Rabban Gamaliel the Elder died, there has been no more reverence for the law, and purity and piety died out at the same time" (Tractate Sotah, 9:15).

[8] In 1515, Martin Luther wrote, "It seems incredible that a man would desire to be damned, in order that the damned might be saved."

They are Israelites, and to them belong the adoption, the glory, the covenants, the giving of the law, the worship, and the promises. To them belong the patriarchs, and from their race, according to the flesh, is the Christ,[9] who is God over all, blessed forever. Amen. (Romans 9:4-5)

With his affection for his fellow Jews firmly established, Paul proceeds to lay out a sophisticated theological presentation. He begins by considering how it is possible that Israel, favored with such privileges and having been educated and spent centuries watching for the promised Messiah, did not recognize Him when He came. Did God's promise to Israel fail? "By no means!" Paul answers. Israel did not miss the Messiah due to a failure of God's word (9:6a), but rather, as Paul will demonstrate, because of a hardening of her heart (11:25). Israel had neglected God's blessing through her unbelief.

"For not all who are descended from Israel are Israel" (9:6b). Here the apostle picks up on a distinction he had introduced earlier. In Romans 2:28-29, Paul taught that there have always been two Israels—those physically descended from Jacob and those who were his spiritual offspring. God gave His promise to the latter: "Through Isaac shall your offspring be named" (9:7, quoting Gen 21:12). Moreover, "It is not the children of the flesh who are the children of God, but the children of the promise are counted as offspring" (9:8). As an illustration, Paul points to God's choosing of Abraham's younger son Isaac, rather than his first-born son Ishmael, as the beneficiary of His promise. In His sovereignty, God overruled the traditional cultural norm of the father's inheritance flowing to the first-born son. Isaac was the son of the promise. Likewise, God chose Jacob over Esau "though they were not yet born and had done nothing either good or bad"

---

[9] On this passage, John Calvin notes, "If he honored the whole human race when he connected himself with it by sharing our nature, much more did he honor the Jews, with whom he desired to have a close bond of affinity."

(11:11). Why? So "God's purpose of election might continue, not because of works but because of him who calls" (9:11). Paul points to God's sovereign choosing of the patriarchs of the Jewish faith and shows us His promises did not fail.

Indeed, the Jewish Bible foretold God's plans for Jews and Gentiles: "even us whom he has called, not from the Jews only but also from the Gentiles" (9:24). In 9:25-26, the apostle quotes two passages from the prophet Hosea to demonstrate God's preexistent plan to include the Gentiles in His family. And in 9:27-29, he cites two texts from Isaiah that tell us God planned to reduce the number of Jews in His family to a remnant. Theologian John Stott notes:

> By bringing the Hosea and Isaiah texts together, Paul provides Old Testament warrant for his vision. On the one hand, God has called us, he writes, not only from the Jews but also from the Gentiles (24). So there is a fundamental Jewish-Gentile solidarity in God's new society. On the other hand, Paul is conscious of the serious imbalance between the size of the Gentile participation and the size of the Jewish participation in the redeemed community. As Hosea prophesied, multitudes of Gentiles, formerly disenfranchised, have now been welcomed as the people of God. As Isaiah prophesied, however, the Jewish membership was only a remnant of the nation, so small in fact as to constitute not the inclusion of Israel but it's exclusion, not its acceptance but it's "rejection" (11:15).[10]

Jesus spoke to these affairs in Matt 8:11-12a when He said: "I tell you, many will come from east and west and recline at table with

---

[10] John R. W. Stott, *The Message of Romans* (Downers Grove, IL: Intervarsity Press, 1994), p. 275.

Abraham, Isaac, and Jacob in the kingdom of heaven, while the sons of the kingdom will be thrown into the outer darkness."

Paul then summarizes what would have been seen as an awkward state of affairs by his fellow Jews: "Gentiles who did not pursue righteousness have attained it" (9:30), and the Jews who pursued it never reached it (9:31).[11] He then attributes Israel's failure to her carelessness: "they did not pursue it by faith but as if it were based on works." Paul says Israel has "stumbled over the stumbling stone" (9:32), applying the words of Isaiah to reveal Jesus as "a stone of stumbling, and a rock of offense" (9:33, also see Isa 8:14). In his first letter to the church in Corinth, the apostle expresses the same idea: "For Jews demand signs and Greeks seek wisdom, but we preach Christ crucified, a stumbling block to Jews and folly to Gentiles" (1 Cor 1:22-23).

Peter picks up on this idea, quoting the same passage from Isaiah and adding of unbelieving Israel, "They stumble because they disobey the word, *as they were destined to do*" (1 Pet 2:8, emphasis added). Indeed, Israel's rejection of her Messiah was foretold in the Hebrew Bible. In Matthew 21:42, Jesus applies the words of Psalm 118:22 to Himself: "The stone that the builders rejected has become the cornerstone." The promised *Mashiach* that the Jewish religious leaders rejected had become the foundation of God's new covenant. Peter develops this idea in his address to the Jewish council in Jerusalem. They demanded to know by whose power Peter and John had healed the lame man at the temple gate:

> Then Peter, filled with the Holy Spirit, said to them, "Rulers of the people and elders, if we are being examined today concerning a good deed done to a crippled man, by

---

[11] Even today, Jews who claim faith in Jesus make up a tiny minority of both Israel and Christendom.

what means this man has been healed, let it be known to all of you and to all the people of Israel that by the name of Jesus Christ of Nazareth, whom you crucified, whom God raised from the dead—by him this man is standing before you well. This Jesus is the stone that was rejected by you, the builders, which has become the cornerstone." (Acts 4:8-11)

Peter elsewhere refers to Jesus as "a living stone rejected by men but in the sight of God chosen and precious" (1 Pet 2:4) and applies Psalm 118:22 to Him (1 Pet 2:7). The theme appears again in Paul's letter to the Ephesians:

So then you are no longer strangers and aliens, but you are fellow citizens with the saints and members of the household of God, built on the foundation of the apostles and prophets, Christ Jesus himself being the cornerstone, in whom the whole structure, being joined together, grows into a holy temple in the Lord. (Ephesians 2:19-21)

In Romans 10, although Israel's prophesied denial of Christ had come to pass, Paul does not doubt Israel's earnestness. He acknowledges their "zeal for God," which he knows from personal experience. Yet, he reveals that their devotion is "not according to knowledge" (10:2). In particular, Israel was ignorant of God's righteousness. Instead, she sought to establish her own righteousness through the works of the law (10:3). Furthermore, Paul indicates that when it comes to salvation, the law and Jesus are opposing alternatives. Righteousness is not achieved through the law but faith and is available to everyone, not just Israel (10:5-13). Paul then makes what would have been an astounding declaration to his Jewish readers. He teaches that, in Christ, there is "no distinction between Jew and Gentile"

(10:12).[12] Indeed, distinctions of race, gender, culture, class, and so on have been rendered irrelevant by Jesus.

So why has Israel not believed? Did she not hear the message of Jesus? Or maybe she didn't understand it? No, that's not it. (10:18-19). Instead, Paul says the reason for Israel's unbelief was her stubbornness. Of the Gentiles, God declared, "I have been found by those who did not seek me" (Rom 10:20; Isa 65:1). Here God's grace is writ large. He allowed Himself to be found by a people who not only did not serve Him but were not even looking for Him. And to His beloved Israel, His hands were continuously outstretched like a Father pleading for the return of a recalcitrant child. "All day long I have held out my hands to a disobedient and contrary people" (10:21; Isa 65:2).

In Romans 11, Paul examines the implications of Israel's disobedience. He teaches that a remnant of Israel endures despite her unbelief. And further, there will be an Israelite recovery in the future, resulting in blessings for all nations. Paul asks and answers two rhetorical questions. First, "Has God rejected his people? By no means!" (11:1). Paul teaches that the Jewish people have prominence or priority in terms of the Good News of Jesus. Earlier in Romans, he taught that the Gospel is "first for the Jew, and also for the Greek" (1:16). At the same time, because God had given Israel a special revelation, He will hold her all the more accountable. Judgment, too, will come "to the Jew first and also the Greek" (2:9). In chapter 11, Paul teaches that while a believing remnant of Israel endures, most have been hardened.

Second, Paul asks, "Did [Israel] stumble in order that they might fall? By no means!" (11:11a). He goes on to explain that through Israel's transgression, salvation has come to the Gentiles. God allowed this to happen "to make Israel jealous" (11:11b). The apostle tells us

---

[12] Paul reiterates this teaching in several other places including: Romans 3:30; Galatians 3:28-29, 5:6, 6:15; 1 Corinthians 12:13.

that Israel's envy of the Gentiles will ultimately lead to her conversion. He declares, "I am an apostle to the Gentiles, I magnify my ministry in order somehow to make my fellow Jews jealous, and thus save some of them" (11:13-14). And Paul includes a note of hope for Israel's future: "Now if their trespass means riches for the world, and if their failure means riches for the Gentiles, how much more will their full inclusion mean!" (11:12).

Stepping back, we see that Paul has laid out a four-part, Israel-centric chain of cosmic events:

1. Through Israel's trespass, salvation came to the Gentiles, which;
2. will arouse the jealousy of Israel, which;
3. will lead to her restoration, which, in due time;
4. will bring even greater riches to the world.

Paul further reveals that Israel's rejection will ultimately mean "the reconciliation of the world" (11:14). This idea of reconciliation, especially regarding Jews and Gentiles, is echoed elsewhere in the New Testament. In Ephesians 2, Paul explains that the Gentiles were once "separated from Christ, alienated from the commonwealth of Israel and strangers to the covenants of promise" (2:12). But they have now been "brought near [to God] by the blood of Christ" (2:13), who broke down "the dividing wall of hostility" (2:14) between Jews and Gentiles. Indeed, Christ's work on the cross served to "create in himself one new man in place of the two" (2:15) so he "might reconcile [Jew and Gentile] to God in one body through the cross, thereby killing the hostility" (2:16) between them. This is why Paul tells the Gentile believers they "are no longer strangers and aliens, but you are fellow citizens with the saints and members of the household of God" (2:19).

This theme also appears in Galatians:

> For in Christ Jesus you are all sons of God, through faith. For as many of you as were baptized into Christ have put on Christ. There is neither Jew nor Greek, there is neither slave nor free, there is no male and female, for you are all one in Christ Jesus. And if you are Christ's, then you are Abraham's offspring, heirs according to promise. (Galatians 3:26-29)

This same spirit of reconciliation and unity between believing Jews and Gentiles is behind the metaphor Paul turns to next in Romans 11. To illustrate his message, the apostle uses the allegory of an olive tree, a recognized symbol of the nation of Israel in Scripture.[13] The tree represents the people of God. Its roots are the patriarchs of the Jewish faith, and its trunk and branches are the historical continuity of faith in God. Paul argues, "if the root is holy, so are the branches" (11:16). He continues:

> But if some of the branches were broken off [unbelieving Jews], and you [Gentiles], although a wild olive shoot, were grafted in among the others and now share in the nourishing root of the olive tree, do not be arrogant toward the branches [believing Jews]. (Romans 11:17-18a, bracketed comments added)

Paul further warns the Gentile believers, "remember it is not you who support the root, but the root that supports you" (11:18b). He further admonishes them: "do not become proud, but fear. For if God did not spare the natural branches [Jews], neither will he spare you [Gentiles]" (11:20-21a, bracketed comments added). Finally, Paul again alludes to the hope and victory that exists for the future of Israel:

---

[13] Jeremiah 11:16; Hosea 14:6.

"And even [the Jews], if they do not continue in their unbelief, will be grafted in, for God has the power to graft them in again" (11:23).

In Paul's day, although Jews were tolerated and protected by law, they nonetheless suffered hatred and even violence at the hands of Gentiles. E. M. Smallwood, a noted professor of Romano-Jewish History, holds that the Jews resisted assimilation into Roman culture, and it was this exclusiveness that bred unpopularity. "The Jew was a figure of amusement, contempt, or hatred to the Gentiles among whom he lived."[14] Here in Romans 11, Paul admonishes the believing Gentiles in Rome to take no part in such persecution of the Jewish people. Indeed, he teaches that Jewish and Gentile believers in Christ are part of the same spiritual family tree.

Paul closes out Romans 11 with a look at the mystery of how Israel's salvation will come about in the end times. He reports, "a partial hardening has come upon Israel until the fullness of the Gentiles has come in" (11:25b). This hardening may be what Jesus had in mind when He said, "Jerusalem will be trampled underfoot by the Gentiles until the times of the Gentiles are fulfilled" (Luke 21:24).[15] While Israel remains hardened and continues to reject Christ, the Gospel will be preached throughout the world,[16] and the Gentiles will respond to it. "And in this way, all Israel will be saved" (11:26a). In other words, the Jews will ultimately find salvation in Christ. N. T. Wright notes, "Paul is envisaging a steady flow of Jews into the church, by grace through faith."[17]

---

[14] E. M. Smallwood, *The Jews under Roman Rule from Pompeii to Diocletian* (Leiden, 1976), p. 123.
[15] "Jesus could be referring to the end of Roman oppression or to the end of the present age, before God's reign is experienced in fullness." (John D Barry et al., *Faithlife Study Bible: Intriguing Insights to Inform Your Faith* (Grand Rapids, Michigan: Zondervan, 2012), Luke 21:24.).
[16] See Mark 13:10; Revelation 7:9 and following.
[17] N T Wright, *The Climax of the Covenant: Christ and the Law in Pauline Theology* (New York: T & T Clark, 2004), p. 233.

The apostle's message is clear: there is only one olive tree and it is comprised of both Jewish and Gentile believers. Nevertheless, Paul does not shy away from the paradox found in the current state of affairs. He cautions the Gentiles, "As regards the Gospel, [the Jews] are enemies[18] for your sake. But as regards election, they are beloved for the sake of their forefathers" (11:28). With regard to the Jews being "enemies," theologian Robert Jamieson explains, "that is, they are regarded and treated [by God] as enemies (in a state of exclusion through unbelief, from the family of God) for the benefit of you Gentiles." Paul adds that in the same way the Gentiles were once disobedient but now receive God's mercy, so too, disobedient Jews will receive mercy (11:30-31). John Stott summarizes:

> On the one hand, the Jews are not only rejecting the gospel but actively opposing it and doing their best to prevent you Gentiles from hearing it. So then, in relation to the gospel, and for your sake (because God wants you to hear and believe), he is hostile to them. On the other hand, the Jews are the chosen, special people of God, the descendants of the noble patriarchs with whom the covenant was made, and to whom the promises were given. So then, in relation to election, and for the sake of the patriarchs (because God is faithful to his covenant and promises), he loves them and is determined to bring them to salvation.[19]

JESUS AND THE JEWS

We now turn from the teachings of Paul to the biblical witness of Jesus' posture toward the Jewish people. Here we find a notable contrast.

---

[18] Jamieson et al., 1997, p. 250.
[19] Stott, 1994, p. 306.

While Jesus' earthly ministry almost exclusively focused on saving the house of Israel, His only clashes, as recorded in Scripture, were with Jewish religious leaders. Let's look at both sides of this issue.

Focus on Israel

Author Trevin Wax notes that, "[Jesus'] ministry appears to be focused so relentlessly on the Jewish people that many scholars have debated whether Jesus was concerned with outsiders at all."[20] In Matthew, Jesus instructs His disciples to avoid the towns of the Gentiles, "but go rather to the lost sheep of the house of Israel" (Matt 10:6). An emphasis on the Jewish people is also evident in His prophetic warnings to the nation of Israel,[21] and the symbolic actions He took, such as cleansing the temple[22] and cursing the fig tree.[23] Jesus' Israel-centric approach is perhaps expressed most clearly in the story of the Gentile woman who begged Him to help her demon-possessed daughter:

> But he did not answer her a word. And his disciples came and begged him, saying, "Send her away, for she is crying out after us."
>
> He answered, "I was sent only to the lost sheep of the house of Israel." But she came and knelt before him, saying, "Lord, help me."
>
> And he answered, "It is not right to take the children's bread and throw it to the dogs."

---

[20] Trevin Wax, "Why Did Jesus Say He Came Only for Israel?" The Gospel Coalition, January 28, 2013, www.thegospelcoalition.org/blogs/trevin-wax/why-did-jesus-say-he-came-only-for-israel/.

[21] Matthew 24; Mark 13; Luke 13:6-9, 21.

[22] Mark 11:15-19. See also Matthew 21:12-17; Luke 19:45-48; John 2:13-16.

[23] Mark 11:12-14, 20-25. See also Matthew 21:18-22.

She said, "Yes, Lord, yet even the dogs eat the crumbs that fall from their masters' table."

Then Jesus answered her, "O woman, great is your faith! Be it done for you as you desire." And her daughter was healed instantly. (Matthew 15:23-28)

In this passage, Jesus unmistakably reveals His primary focus is on the Jewish people. He refers to His ministry and message as the bread of the children of Israel and suggests it is not right to throw that bread to the Gentile "dogs." However, because of the woman's faith, He heals her daughter. First to the Jew, but also the Gentile (Rom 1:16).

Conflicts with Jewish Religious Leaders

The New Testament contains no record of Jesus clashing with anyone other than Jewish religious leaders: the Scribes, Pharisees, Chief Priests, and Teachers of the Law. He does not quarrel with Jewish laypeople, or the Gentiles, or even the Romans who carried out His execution. Historian Everett Ferguson notes:

> During Jesus' ministry in Galilee his principal religious opposition came from the Pharisees over the interpretation of the law of Moses applied to matters of daily life. At Jerusalem the opposition came from the Sadducees, the leading priests and ruling aristocrats who controlled the temple and matters related to it.[24]

The conflict between Jesus and Jewish leaders went both ways, though not to the same degree. On the one hand, Jewish authorities persecuted Jesus, ultimately to the point of death. On the other hand, Jesus castigated many Jewish leaders for their hypocrisy and blindness.

---

[24] Ferguson, 2013, pp. 30-31.

One could (perhaps crudely) summarize the conflict recorded in the New Testament as follows: The message of the Christians to the Jews was "repent and be saved by placing your faith in Jesus, your Messiah." The message of the Jews to the Christians was "renounce your heresy or die." We will examine both sides of this conflict.

The Jewish Persecution of Jesus

Luke 4 records Jesus' revelation about Himself at the start of His ministry. In a Nazareth synagogue, He stood and read from the scroll of Isaiah:

> The Spirit of the Lord is on me,
> because he has anointed me
> to proclaim good news to the poor.
> He has sent me to proclaim freedom for the prisoners
> and recovery of sight for the blind,
> to set the oppressed free,
> to proclaim the year of the Lord's favor.
> (Luke 4:8-9, Isaiah 61:1-2)

Jesus then pronounced, "Today this Scripture has been fulfilled in your hearing" (Luke 4:21). His fellow Jews initially "spoke well of him and marveled at the gracious words that were coming from his mouth" (4:22). However, as He kept speaking, the people grew angry. Here in the middle of a Jewish synagogue on the Sabbath, Jesus was teaching that the Gentiles would receive God's help while Israel had to suffer.[25] Consequently,

> When they heard these things, all in the synagogue were
> filled with wrath. And they rose up and drove him out of
> the town and brought him to the brow of the hill on which

---

[25] John D Barry et al., *Faithlife Study Bible: Intriguing Insights to Inform Your Faith* (Grand Rapids, Michigan: Zondervan, 2012), Luke 4:21.

their town was built so that they could throw him down the cliff. (Luke 4:28-29)

Thus began the Jewish persecution of Jesus that continued even after His death. The nature of Jesus' persecution ranged from questioning, testing, and challenging to arresting and beating and ultimately having Him killed.[26] And His apostles, disciples, and followers inherited the hatred their Lord's teachings had stirred up. Jesus knew this persecution would come: "If they persecuted me, they will also persecute you" (John 15:20). He warned His followers to prepare them for what lay in store:

> They will lay their hands on you and persecute you, delivering you up to the synagogues and prisons, and you will be brought before kings and governors for my name's sake . . . You will be delivered up even by parents and brothers and relatives and friends, and some of you they will put to death. You will be hated by all for my name's sake. (Luke 21:12, 16-17)[27]

It should be noted that in the first incident mentioned above, Jesus' persecutors were described as "all who were in the synagogue" (Luke 4:28). After that, Scripture records His persecution coming solely at the hands of Jewish religious leaders. It is also important to recognize that not every interaction Christ had with Jewish authorities was contentious. For example, the apostle John reported a division among the Jewish religious leaders concerning Jesus:

---

[26] See Appendix A: Instances of the Persecution of Jesus as Recorded in the Gospels.
[27] See also Luke 12:11-12; John 16:2-3.

Many even of the authorities believed in him, but for fear
of the Pharisees they did not confess it so that they would
not be put out of the synagogue. (John 12:42)[28]

The presence of such a disparity among the Jewish authorities tells
us their opposition to Jesus was not unanimous. Indeed, only a portion
of Jewish religious leadership—albeit the highest-ranking segment—
was behind His persecution.

Jesus' Rebuking of Jewish Religious Leaders

For His part, Jesus issued a series of forceful denunciations of the
scribes and Pharisees, which has come to be known as the "Woes of
the Pharisees."[29] In these passages, Jesus takes the religious leaders to
task for their hypocrisy, portraying them as preoccupied with the ritual
observance of minor details. He accused them of putting on an outer
shell of piety while keeping their hearts far from God. His language is
strong and convicting:

Woe to you, scribes and Pharisees, hypocrites! For you are
like whitewashed tombs, which outwardly appear
beautiful, but within are full of dead people's bones and all
uncleanness. So you also outwardly appear righteous to
others, but within you are full of hypocrisy and
lawlessness. (Matthew 23:27-28)

In these woes, Jesus brands some of the Jewish leaders as
"hypocrites" and "blind fools." He accuses them of traveling "across
sea and land to make a single proselyte, and when he becomes a
proselyte, you make him twice as much a child of hell as yourselves"
(Matt 23:15b). And He asks rhetorically, "You serpents, you brood of

---

[28] See also John 9:16, 10:19-21.
[29] See Matthew 23:1–39; Mark 12:35–40; Luke 11:37–54, 20:45–47.

vipers, how are you to escape being sentenced to hell?" (Matt 23:33).
Jesus again clashes with the Pharisees in John 8:

> Jesus said to them, "If God were your Father, you would
> love me, for I came from God and I am here. I came not
> of my own accord, but he sent me. Why do you not
> understand what I say? It is because you cannot bear to
> hear my word. You are of your father the devil, and your
> will is to do your father's desires. He was a murderer from
> the beginning, and does not stand in the truth, because
> there is no truth in him. When he lies, he speaks out of his
> own character, for he is a liar and the father of lies." (John
> 8:42-44)

Jesus' judgment on Israel and her leaders was not limited to His
words. He also expressed His righteous anger through symbolic
actions, such as the cleansing of the temple.[30] Scholar Walter Wessel
describes the importance of where that incident is placed in Scripture:

> The temple cleansing is sandwiched between the two
> incidents of the fig tree, an arrangement meant to link the
> accounts. The judgment symbolized by the cursing of the
> fig tree is initiated by Jesus' cleansing of the temple, and
> the cleansing of the temple is prophetic of the destruction
> of Jerusalem and the eschatological [end times] judgment
> (cf. Mark 13).[31]

Notice that Jesus was not arguing against the Jews as God's chosen
people or against Israel as a nation. Instead, His problem was with
Jewish leaders who did not correctly understand their own Scriptures.
The target of His criticism was their elevation of manmade

---

[30] Mark 11:15-19. See also Matt 21:12-17; Luke 19:45-48, John 2:13-16.
[31] W. W. Wessel, *The Expositor's Bible Commentary*, ed. F. E. Gaebelein, vol. 8 (Grand Rapids:
Zondervan Publishing House, 1984), p. 727.

interpretations above the actual Hebrew Scriptures, thus leading His people astray. Indeed, Christ's ire was not raised against the *Jewishness* of these religious leaders but rather their disloyalty to both Scripture and God. As He told the Sadducees who asked Him a misguided question about the resurrection, "You are wrong because you know neither the Scriptures nor the power of God" (Matt 22:29).

It's essential to recognize that Jesus' woes and prophetic warnings are no more anti-Jewish than the judgments found in the Hebrew Bible. God Himself refers to Israel as an unfaithful bride,[32] a stiff-necked people,[33] and a disobedient and rebellious nation.[34] Indeed, Israel was so incessantly disobedient that God disciplined her with slavery, forty years of wandering in the wilderness, death, exile, and at the advent of Christ, a hardening.[35]

Equally important is the *reason* God disciplines Israel: it is because He loves her.[36] The psalmist writes, "Blessed is the one you discipline, Lord, the one you teach from your law" (Ps 94:12). The author of Hebrews teaches that "the Lord disciplines the one he loves, and he chastens everyone he accepts as his son" (Heb 12:6). And the Lord Himself tells us, "Those whom I love I rebuke and discipline" (Rev 3:19a).

It is also important to acknowledge that neither Jesus' clashes with religious leaders nor His teachings were aimed at negating the Hebrew Scriptures. "Do not think that I have come to abolish the Law or the Prophets; I have not come to abolish them but to fulfill them" (Matt 5:17). His focus was on clarifying, and in some instances, elevating the teachings of the *Tanakh*.[37] This sense of elevation is evident in the

---

[32] Jeremiah 31:32

[33] Exodus 32:9, 33:3-5, 2 Chronicles 30:8

[34] Isaiah 65:1-4

[35] Exodus 1; Numbers 14:34, 21:6; 2 Kings 17:23.

[36] Deuteronomy 4:37, 7:7-8, 10:15; 1 Kings 10:9; Psalm 47:4, 78:68, 87:2; Hosea 3:1, 11:1; Malachi 1:2-3.

[37] *Tanakh* is the Jewish name for the Hebrew Bible. This sis the same body of text Christians know as the Old Testament. *Tanakh* is an acronym made up of the first Hebrew letter of each of

Sermon on the Mount in which Jesus issued a series of *"You have heard that it was said . . . but I say to you"* statements on anger, lust, oaths, retaliation, and loving your enemies.[38]

THOSE WHO DENY CHRIST

There is one final area of New Testament teaching we need to look at because of its relevance to our study. The ultimate source of conflict between Jews and Christians is the person of Christ. The Gospel of Jesus hinges on accepting His work as our divine messiah. Therefore, any theology that denies Him—Jewish or otherwise—must be opposed as a false teaching that ultimately leads to damnation. The apostle Peter warned of the high stakes involved:

> There will be false teachers among you, who will secretly bring in destructive heresies, even denying the Master who bought them, bringing upon themselves swift destruction. And many will follow their sensuality, and because of them the way of truth will be blasphemed. (2 Peter 2:1b-2)

Jesus unequivocally teaches us that:

> Everyone who acknowledges me before men, I also will acknowledge before my Father who is in heaven, but whoever denies me before men, I also will deny before my Father who is in heaven. (Matthew 10:32-33)

And again:

---

the three subdivisions of books: T for *Torah*, which means "teaching, instruction," N for *Nevi'im*, which means "prophets," and K for *Ketuvim*, which means "writings." Together, the letters TNK are pronounced *ta-NAK*.

[38] Matthew 5:21-48.

For whoever is ashamed of me and of my words in this adulterous and sinful generation, of him will the Son of Man also be ashamed when he comes in the glory of his Father with the holy angels. (Mark 8:38)[39]

These sober warnings apply to anyone who denies Christ. That includes His fellow Jews who refuse Him as their Messiah. Scripture does not leave us any wiggle room on this issue. As followers of Christ, we cannot accept any theology which denies Him, including modern Judaism.

NEW TESTAMENT SUMMARY

Let's summarize what we've discovered in the New Testament writings. The words of Jesus and the teachings of His apostle Paul have marked out the essential elements of a biblical view of Jews and Judaism from a Christian perspective. And what we find is not a narrow us-versus-them approach. Instead, a biblical view is a nuanced view in which we must hold several ideas in tension. First, we need to operate from a foundation of love for the Jewish people and an earnest desire for their salvation. At the same time, we have to acknowledge that some Jews have denied Christ and been disloyal to Scripture and to God. The New Testament is clear about this. On the other hand, Scripture is also explicit about Israel's central role in God's great story of redemption and about and her future salvation. This balanced biblical posture can be captured in the following five-part framework. The New Testament teaches that Christians are to:

1. Recognize Israel's central role in God's story
2. Acknowledge the failure of Jewish religious leadership
3. Reject Jewish teachings that deny Christ

---

[39] See also Luke 12:8-9; 1 John 2:23; 2 Timothy 2:12.

4. Understand Israel's future salvation

5. Love and earnestly desire the salvation of Jews

We will look at each of these five points in more detail. But first, it is essential to recognize that, in addition to this framework, which speaks specifically to Jewish-Christian relations, the New Testament has a lot to say about how Christians ought to treat others in general. These are instructions that apply to everyone, Jews included. Jesus taught us to "Love your enemies and pray for those who persecute you, so that you may be sons of your Father who is in heaven" (Matt 5:44-45). The apostle Paul said we are to "Do nothing from selfish ambition or conceit, but in humility count others more significant than yourselves" (Phil 2:3). And "If possible, so far as it depends on you, live peaceably with all" (Rom 12:18). In the Sermon on the Mount, Jesus preached radical grace and humility toward others:

> You have heard that it was said, "An eye for an eye and a tooth for a tooth." But I say to you, do not resist the one who is evil. But if anyone slaps you on the right cheek, turn to him the other also. And if anyone would sue you and take your tunic, let him have your cloak as well. And if anyone forces you to go one mile, go with him two miles. Give to the one who begs from you, and do not refuse the one who would borrow from you. (Matthew 5:38-42)

The role of Christians as oppressors, persecutors, or haters of people is patently unbiblical. It is the antithesis of what Christ taught. Instead, the job of the authentic follower of Jesus is to love and serve others. Jesus did not just teach this principle. He modeled it for us.

> But Jesus called them to him and said, "You know that the rulers of the Gentiles lord it over them, and their great ones exercise authority over them. It shall not be so among you.

But whoever would be great among you must be your servant, and whoever would be first among you must be your slave, even as the Son of Man came not to be served but to serve, and to give his life as a ransom for many." (Matthew 20:25-28)

Keeping this biblical basis of love and humility in mind, let's take a closer look at five points of our framework.

1. Christians are to recognize Israel's central role in God's story.

New Testament theology is unquestionably grounded in the Tanakh. The Hebrew Scriptures are the rich historical and theological soil in which Christianity is rooted. And the Jewish NT writers were writing to and for Jews. They stood unabashedly on the shoulders of the giants of the Jewish faith. Jewish Rabbi Samuel Sandmel notes:

> The controversies between Jesus and the Scribes/Pharisees have no referent outside the community of Israel; Jesus' preaching of the coming kingdom could have had meaning only for Jews; the synagogues in which Jesus reads from the prophets, heals the sick, and forgives sins are Jewish houses of worship for believing Jews and not unconverted gentiles.[40]

The NT authors clearly teach Jesus as the Jewish *Mashiach* (Messiah). And they also teach the priority of the Jewish people in God's eyes. As Jews themselves, the authors undoubtedly regarded Israel as a nation brought about supernaturally and called by God.[41] Consequently, the Gentiles do not replace Israel as God's people but

---

[40] Samuel Sandmel (2005), *A Jewish Understanding of the New Testament* (Woodstock, Vt.: Jewish Lights Pub), p. 90.
[41] Genesis 18:1-21.

are grafted into her (Rom 11). Indeed, it was through Israel that God sovereignly chose to bring the good news of salvation to the world. "Salvation is from the Jews" (John 4:22b).

In the Jewish Bible, God appointed Israel as a priest and a light to the nations. However, Israel fell into the idolatrous ways of the nations around her and had to be disciplined. Subsequently, under the New Covenant, God appointed the early Jewish believers—led by the apostle Paul—to bring the Gospel to the Gentiles. Author and teacher Warren Wiersbe identified a beautiful progression in Jewish-Christian relations outlined by the Apostle Paul in Romans 15:

1. The Jews glorify God among the Gentiles (Rom. 15:9; Ps 18:49).
2. The Gentiles rejoice with the Jews (Rom. 15:10; Deut 32:43).
3. All the Jews and Gentiles together praise God (Rom 15:11; Ps 117:1).
4. Christ shall reign over Jews and Gentiles (Rom 15:12; Isa 11:10).[42]

Further evidence of Israel's foundational role in God's story is that the New Testament is saturated with allusions to and citations from the Hebrew Bible.[43] As we saw above, Paul relied on numerous passages from the Tanakh to build his case to the believers in Rome. This reveals a fundamental theological continuity between the Hebrew Bible and the New Testament. Indeed, the NT writers as a whole base their arguments on the Jewish Bible. The phrase "it is written" occurs more than sixty times in the New Testament, each referring to the Tanakh. Even the *Universal Jewish Encyclopedia* acknowledges that "The New

---

[42] Warren W Wiersbe, *The Wiersbe Bible Study Series. Romans 1:18–3:20* (Colorado Springs, Co: David C. Cook, 2011).

[43] There are over 280 direct quotations from the Jewish Bible in the NT. Professor Chris Harrison and Pastor Christoph Römhild put together a beautiful data visualization of the more than 63,000 cross-references they identified between the OT and NT. You can view it at: www.chrisharrison.net/index.php/Visualizations/BibleViz

Testament is regarded by Christians as the fulfillment of the prophecies and the teachings contained in the Old."[44]

In the same way that Paul describes Jews and Gentiles as part of the same tree in Romans 11, the New Testament authors as a whole reveal the Old and New Testaments are two parts of the same redemptive story. The tie that binds the narrative together—indeed the plotline around which the entire story revolves—is Christ. He is the savior promised in the Garden (Gen 3:15), the blessing to all families of the earth guaranteed to Abraham (Gen 12:3), the prophet greater than Moses (Deut 18:15-19), the light for the nations bringing salvation to the ends of the earth (Isa 49:6), and the promised Messiah and King from the line of David and the tribe of Judah (2 Sam 7).[45] The New Testament unmistakably portrays Jesus as the long-awaited *Mashiach* prophesied in the Hebrew Bible and for whom the Jewish people had been waiting for centuries (Luke 2:25; 3:15).

Indeed, Jesus was a Jew raised in a Jewish family in a Jewish town who lived a life of perfect obedience to the Jewish law.[46] The New Testament tells us Jesus was a rabbi with Jewish disciples.[47] He spoke in synagogues, regularly visited the temple, and predominantly traveled in Jewish areas. Moreover, He self-identified as the fulfillment of the Hebrew Scriptures. "And beginning with Moses and all the Prophets, he interpreted to them in all the Scriptures the things concerning himself" (Luke 24:27).[48] Thus, the New Testament proclaims itself not just Jewish in essence but a fulfillment and continuation of the Hebrew Scriptures.

We need to hold this Judeo-centric understanding of the Gospel story in tension with the OT prophecies that Israel would fail when the

---

[44] Landman & Cohen, 1969, vol. 8, p. 174.
[45] See also 1 Chronicles 17:11-14; 2 Chronicles 6:16.
[46] Luke 2:27; Galatians 4:4.
[47] Matthew 26:25, 26:49; Mark 9:5, 10:51, 11:21, 14:45; John 1:49, 3:2, 4:31, 6:25, 9:2, 11:8.
[48] See also John 1:45, 5:46; Acts 8:35, 13:27.

Messiah arrived. As we saw in Romans 9-11, it was God's plan all along that the Gospel of Christ would be given to Gentiles where it would flourish. Indeed, Jesus' command to "make disciples of all nations" (Matt 28:19) flowed directly from God's promise to Abraham that "in you, *all* the families of the earth shall be blessed" (Gen 12:3, emphasis added). The Jews are, indeed, God's chosen people. Israel is the nation He called forth from Sarah's womb and the channel through which He brought salvation to mankind. However, His story was never intended to include *only* Israel.

2. Christians are to acknowledge the failure of Jewish religious leadership.

While we must not diminish the importance of Israel, her failures at Christ's arrival cannot be marginalized. Jewish leaders had become disloyal to Scripture and disobedient to God. As a result, the religious leaders failed to recognize their own Messiah and instead brought about His death. The apostle Peter expressed this notion explicitly in his sermon to the Jews gathered in Jerusalem on the day of Pentecost:

> This Jesus, delivered up according to the definite plan and foreknowledge of God, you crucified and killed by the hands of lawless men. (Acts 2:23)

Indeed, through Israel's transgression, they were partially hardened, and salvation came to the Gentiles. This is the scenario foretold in the Hebrew Bible. And this state of affairs continues today as rabbinic Judaism endures in not only denying but opposing Christ.

3. Christians are to reject Jewish teachings that deny Christ.

Paul modeled the ideal Christian posture toward Jews. He held his love for the Jewish people and his desire for their salvation alongside his bold refutation of the parts of Jewish theology that reject Christ. Jesus and the New Testament authors of one accord taught this balance as the proper attitude of Christians toward Jews. As we looked at above, the warnings in Scripture against denying Christ are grave. And they apply to Jew and Gentile alike. Consider the stern words of the apostle John:

> Who is the liar but he who denies that Jesus is the Christ? This is the antichrist, he who denies the Father and the Son. No one who denies the Son has the Father. Whoever confesses the Son has the Father also. (1 John 2:22-23)

4. Christians are to understand Israel's future salvation.

Paul provided an end-times perspective of the mystery of Israel's salvation. He taught that "a partial hardening has come upon Israel until the fullness of the Gentiles has come in" (Rom 11:25b). And in the meantime, the Gospel will be preached throughout the world.[49] The Gentiles will respond to it, "and in this way, all Israel will be saved" (11:26a). Thus, as theologian Charles Hodge notes, "the rejection of the Jews was neither total nor final."[50] While the New Testament writers left the specific details a mystery, their teaching is clear: the Jewish people have a future in God's Kingdom.

5. Christians are to love and earnestly desire the salvation of the Jewish people.

Given the amount of persecution Jesus endured during His earthly ministry, it is not unreasonable to imagine He may have had his fellow

---

[49] See Mark 13:10; Rev 7:9 and following.
[50] Charles H. Hodge, *The Geneva Series of Commentaries* (United Kingdom: Banner of Truth Trust, 1974), p. 353.

Jews in mind when He commanded His followers to "love your enemies and pray for those who persecute you" (Matt 5:44). Paul modeled this divine mandate in the "great sorrow and anguish" (Rom 9:2) he felt for his fellow Jews and his earnest desire for their salvation (Rom 10:1). Further, in his illustration of the olive tree, Paul admonishes Christians to take no part in anti-Jewish attitudes. Christians wanting to adopt a biblical attitude toward Jews must do the same.

TWO THEOLOGICAL MARKERS

With the New Testament perspective on Jews and Judaism established, let's turn to its teachings on two somewhat controversial Jewish-Christian matters. The first is the Sabbath versus the Lord's Day. Are Christians to gather on the last day of the week (Saturday) in obedience to the Torah commandments about the Sabbath? Or should we gather on the first day of the week (Sunday), as the Lord's Day? The second issue we'll look at is Passover versus Easter. Are believers to keep Passover or Easter? Or maybe both? These issues are discussed in the New Testament, in the writings of the early Christians, and at the council of Nicaea. They can help us by serving as trackable markers that reveal the degree and nature of anti-Jewish impact on Christian theology throughout the historical era we are examining.

Sabbath/The Lord's Day

The Sabbath is alluded to twice in the Old Testament before it becomes part of the Law given at Mount Sinai. First, the "seventh day" is mentioned in Gen 2:2 as the day God rested from His creation of the world. And later, as Moses led the Israelites through the wilderness after the Exodus from Egypt, the Sabbath was commanded in connection with God's gift of manna (Ex 16:23-29). This declaration included a mandate: "Six days you shall gather it, but on the seventh day, which is a Sabbath, there will be none" (Ex 16:26). It was a test of Israel's obedience, which she promptly failed:

> On the seventh day some of the people went out to gather, but they found none. And the Lord said to Moses, "How long will you refuse to keep my commandments and my laws? See! The Lord has given you the Sabbath; therefore, on the sixth day he gives you bread for two days. Remain each of you in his place; let no one go out of his place on the seventh day." So, the people rested on the seventh day. (Exodus 16:27-30)

Later at Mount Sinai, the *Shabbat* (Sabbath) was given to Israel as part of the Law of Moses. It is the fourth of the Ten Commandments.[51] The Tanakh includes prescriptive teachings about the Sabbath, warning Israel to remember it and keep it holy:[52] do no work,[53] carry no load,[54] make your offerings,[55] and do not desecrate it.[56] During the intertestamental period,[57] the Sabbath took on an even more legalistic interpretation. In an attempt to build "fences" around the Torah, Jewish teachers developed at least thirty-nine extra-biblical forms of activities that they forbid on the Sabbath. These included walking more than 1,000 cubits, drawing water into any container, wearing perfume, and helping an animal out of a pit. Such was the view of the Sabbath held in first-century Jewish culture into which Jesus was born.

Interestingly, although nine of the Ten Commandments are either repeated verbatim or endorsed in the New Testament, the

---

[51] Exodus 20:8-11; Deuteronomy 5:12-15.
[52] Exodus 20:8; Deuteronomy 5:12; Jeremiah 17:24; Ezekiel 20:19-20.
[53] Exodus 20:10, 31:15, 35:2; Leviticus 23:3,
[54] Jeremiah 17:21-22, 27.
[55] 1 Chronicles 23:31, 2:4, 8:13, 31:3.
[56] Exodus 31:14, Nehemiah 13:17-18, Isaiah 56:2, Ezekiel 20:13-24, 22:8, 23:38.
[57] This is the roughly 400-year period of history after the Old Testament was closed and before Jesus arrived.

commandment about the Sabbath is not.[58] The significant difference between the Old and New Testaments in their emphases on the Sabbath is nowhere clearly explained. However, since both testaments are part of Holy Scripture, this discrepancy cannot be written off as an accident or an oversight. Under the New Covenant ushered in by Jesus, the emphasis on *Shabbat* must have shifted for a reason. Because the Sabbath predates the Law of Moses, one could argue that it should be viewed as a universal command. In that case, since God gave it before the Law of Moses, the Sabbath would presumably outlast the Law as well. Yet, in his letter to the Colossians, the apostle Paul opposes those who command Sabbath compliance:

> Therefore let no one pass judgment on you in questions of food and drink, or with regard to a festival or a new moon or a Sabbath. These are a shadow of the things to come, but the substance belongs to Christ. (Colossians 2:16-17)

Paul's message to the primarily Gentile church was that they should not let anyone disqualify them based on whether or not they kept the Jewish legal observances such as the Sabbath. Because he listed the Sabbath among other Jewish legal requirements, it is possible Paul was only referring to the legal observance of the Sabbath as required by the Law of Moses and not a pre-existing universal directive. While the keeping of the Sabbath is not explicitly overturned in this passage, it is clearly taught as optional.

Paul's position on the Sabbath in Colossians aligns with the ruling of the Jerusalem Council as recorded in Acts 15:1-29. At that council, Paul, Peter, James, and others gathered to discuss what should be required of new Gentile believers. In a letter indicating their decision, the council wrote:

---

[58] See Appendix B: The Ten Commandments as Referenced in the New Testament.

> For it has seemed good to the Holy Spirit and to us to lay on you no greater burden than these requirements: that you abstain from what has been sacrificed to idols, and from blood, and from what has been strangled, and from sexual immorality. If you keep yourselves from these, you will do well. (Acts 15:28-29)

In this passage, the New Testament unambiguously teaches that observance of the Sabbath is no longer required. That said, the Sabbath clearly still holds significance in the New Testament. Jesus publicly revealed His ministry on the Sabbath (Luke 4:16). He also taught,[59] healed,[60] and even worked[61] on the Sabbath. Likewise, the early Christians regularly gathered in the synagogue on the Sabbath.[62] While the early Jewish Christians kept the Sabbath, it was also a frequent matter of contention between Jesus and the religious leaders. Indeed,

> In the New Testament, the Sabbath is referred to more often as a source of controversy than a commandment to be kept. More than half of the time any New Testament author mentions the Sabbath, it is as a source of conflict between Yeshua[63] and the Jewish religious leaders. And in one hundred percent of the passages where Yeshua teaches about the Sabbath, He is clashing with Jewish leaders over it.[64]

Consider the incident in which the Pharisees chastised Jesus for allowing his disciples to pluck heads of grain on the Sabbath.

---

[59] Matthew 12:1-12; Mark 1:21, 2:23-28, 6:2, Luke 6:1-9, 13:10-16.
[60] Luke 4:31-37, 14:1-5; John 5:9, 9:14.
[61] John 5:16-17.
[62] Acts 13:14, 13:44, 17:2, 18:4.
[63] *Yeshua* is our Lord's name in Hebrew. It means "salvation." *Yeshua* and *Jesus* refer to the same Person.
[64] R. L. Solberg, *Torahism: Are Christians Required to Keep the Law of Moses?* (Williamson College Press, 2019), p. 84

And He said to them, "The Sabbath was made for man, not man for the Sabbath. So the Son of Man is lord even of the Sabbath." (Mark 2:27-28)

What did this enigmatic statement mean? There are at least two points we can glean from it. First, the extra-biblical prohibitions introduced by the Pharisees had distorted God's original intention for the Sabbath. In this passage, Jesus is telling the Pharisees that their Sabbath regulations are manmade additions to God's requirements and, therefore, not mandatory. In other words, Jesus is defending the actions of His disciples as consistent with the true intention of the Sabbath. He used this opportunity to clarify the original purpose of the Sabbath as given in the Torah.

Second, Jesus' declaration that the Sabbath "was made for man, not man for the Sabbath" harkens back to Genesis 2:2 and the role of the seventh day in creation. It suggests the Sabbath was given to humanity not as an essential mandate but as a blessing—a "holy rhythm" of rest and restoration first modeled by God. It also brings to mind Jesus' response to the Jews who were persecuting Him for healing a man on the Sabbath: "But Jesus answered them, 'My Father is working until now, and I am working'" (John 5:17). Jamieson's commentary on the phrase "and I work" in this verse is insightful:

> The "I" is emphatic; "The creative and conservative activity of My Father has known no sabbath-cessation from the beginning until now, and that is the law of My working."[65]

Because God Himself works on the Sabbath, doing so cannot be inherently wrong or sinful. Therefore, the Sabbath requirements given in the Law of Moses—just like the dietary restrictions and the temple

---

[65] Jamieson et al., 1997, p. 136.

laws—should not be viewed as a universal moral directive for all people at all times. Instead, they were given by God for two reasons. First, to set Israel apart from all the nations around her and mark her as God's own people. Second, the Sabbath requirements were given as a test of Israel's obedience under the Law.

The twin biblical teachings that the Sabbath (a.) is a directive tied to creation which transcends the Law of Moses and (b.) is not a requirement for Christians (Col 2:16-17)[66] need to be held in tension. The author of Hebrews gives us some additional insight. He explains how the Israelites failed to enter into God's rest (Heb 3:19) and, therefore, "the promise of entering his rest still stands" (Heb 4:1). Thus, believers are now able to enter into a true Sabbath rest. Namely:

> Hebrews 4:11 points to a future rest for those who are obedient. The passage emphasizes the Old Testament principles that God's Sabbath is based on abstinence from work (4:10), rest (4:3), tied to creation (4:4), and a call for obedience (4:6).[67]

Another bit of Scriptural evidence to consider is God's giving of the Sabbath as a sign of the Sinai Covenant.[68] This covenant was ultimately broken by Israel[69] and replaced by a new and superior covenant in Jesus.[70] If the Old Covenant has passed away (Heb 8:13), it stands to reason that the signs given under that covenant have passed away as well. Indeed, the author of Hebrews indicates the legal Sabbath rest— which Paul referred to as "a shadow of the things to

---

[66] According to Jewish law, non-Jews were not in the Covenant and never had been. "They were bound by the Noachide commandments, not by the Torah of Moses. Despite their claims to be the 'true Israel' and 'Abraham's sons through faith,' they were halakhically 'heathen' ('*ovedei kokhavim*)" (Alexander, 1999, p. 6).

[67] Babcock et al., 2016, *Hebrews 4:11*.

[68] Exodus 31:13; Ezekiel 20:12, 17.

[69] Jeremiah 31:32; Hebrews 8:9.

[70] Jeremiah 31:31-34; Hebrews 8:6-13.

come"[71]—has been replaced by a new and superior rest in Jesus (Heb 4:1-11). Consequently, it is not unreasonable to conclude that, like the Sinai Covenant, the Sabbath commandment—at least in the form given in the Law of Moses—was not intended to last forever.

Intriguingly, outside of the Law of Moses, the only commandment God gave regarding the Sabbath was constrained to a specific people and place. The Israelites were not to gather manna on the seventh day of the week as they wandered in the wilderness (Ex 16:23-29). This mandate was obviously not universal, nor is it still binding today. Perhaps there is a transcendent "essence" of Sabbath intended in Scripture, the idea of resting in God at regular intervals as a gift or blessing given by God. Theologians Elwell & Beitzel note,

> The Scriptures relate that God gave his people the Sabbath as an opportunity to serve him, and as a reminder of two great truths in the Bible—creation and redemption."[72]

We've seen how the New Testament took on a new perspective of the Sabbath as a legal obligation. What, then, of the day of its observance? While the Jewish Sabbath was required to be kept on the last day of the week, the New Testament indicates believers had begun gathering on the first day of the week.[73] For example, in Corinthians, Paul reminds his readers to contribute money to the Jerusalem church "on the first day of every week" (1 Cor 16:2). Elwell & Beitzel expound on this passage:

> Why Sunday? Obviously the first day of the week had taken on a special significance among Christians in Corinth before Paul wrote this letter (AD 55–56), and he

---

[71] Colossians 2:16-17.

[72] Walter A Elwell and B. J. Beitzel, *Baker Encyclopedia of the Bible*, vol. 2 (Grand Rapids, Mich.: Baker, 1988), p. 1874.

[73] Many early Jewish believers observed both the Saturday Sabbath and the Lord's Day on the first day of the week.

makes it clear that the observance was not merely local (see 1 Cor 16:1). There was some special "Sunday event" that would make it easy for Christians to remember their obligations to the poor.[74]

In a passage encouraging continued charitable giving (which, as we saw above, Paul indicated was a Sunday occurrence), Paul adds,

For the ministry of this service is not only supplying the needs of the saints but is also overflowing in many thanksgivings to God." (2 Corinthians 9:12)

In this passage, the Greek word rendered "service" is λειτουργία (leitourgia), from which the English word *liturgy* is derived. This word can broadly mean "service" but is elsewhere translated as *ministry*, *offering*, and *worship*. Furthermore, in the book of Acts, Luke describes a Sunday gathering in Troas where Paul spoke for many hours. He talked at such length that a young man named Eutychus nodded off in a deep sleep and dropped out of a third-story window (Acts 20:7-12). This brief passage reveals that a group of Christian believers "had assembled to break bread" (20:7)—a phrase commonly used in the New Testament to refer to the Lord's Supper—and listen to Paul "preach" on a Sunday. Thus, Scripture reveals that very early in the Christian church there were Sunday gatherings where offerings were taken, sermons were preached, and the Lord's Supper was observed. These modern Sunday traditions are all grounded in Scripture.

Another reference to Sunday is found in the book of Revelation, where the apostle John wrote, "I was in the Spirit on the Lord's day, and I heard behind me a loud voice like a trumpet" (Rev 1:10). This is the only use of the phrase "the Lord's day" in the New Testament, and

---

[74] Elwell & Beitzel, 1988, p. 1347.

the text here does not explicitly tie it to the first day of the week. However, we have extra-biblical evidence that the earliest Christians commonly used this phrase in reference to Sunday. As we'll see in the next section, "the Lord's day" is a phrase found in *The Didache*, an ancient Christian writing that was in circulation as early as the 60's. Sunday was the day of the week Christians would devote themselves to the teaching of the Apostles and the fellowship, to the breaking of bread and prayers. Thus, the phrase "The Lord's Day" was in use by Christians by the time John wrote the book of Revelation around AD 95-96.

To recap, the Sabbath, at a minimum, takes on a new understanding in the New Testament. Scripture nowhere explicitly overturns the keeping of the weekly Sabbath or states it has come to an end. At the same time, the New Testament unconditionally teaches that Sabbath observance is not required. (At least not of the Gentiles. And, since, in Christ, there is neither Jew nor Gentile (Gal 3:28), the end of a legal requirement for keeping Sabbath would apply equally to all Christians.)

Regarding the Lord's Day, we see hints that the early church had begun gathering on Sunday. However, Scripture neither requires nor prohibits gathering on the first day of the week. The earliest Christians modeled the nature of Christian gatherings for us. "They devoted themselves to the apostles' teaching and the fellowship, to the breaking of bread and the prayers" (Acts 2:42). And the author of Hebrews taught that meeting together was an essential part of living out our faith:

> And let us consider how to stir up one another to love and good works, not neglecting to meet together, as is the habit of some, but encouraging one another, and all the more as you see the Day drawing near. (Hebrews 10:25)

But it seems that on the matter of which day or how often we ought to gather together, Christians are given freedom in Christ to choose for themselves.

Therefore, the baseline New Testament teaching on the Sabbath versus the Lord's Day can be summed up in the following two points.

1. Keeping the Jewish observance of the Sabbath on the last day of the week is allowed but no longer required.
2. Gathering on the first day of the week is also allowed but not required.

Passover/Easter

There is one sacred Spring season for the Jewish people, *Pesach* (Passover). It was in the midst of this season that Jesus was crucified and resurrected. Not only did His death coincide with the Passover sacrifice, but He was resurrected on the Jewish Day of Firstfruits (*Yom HaBikkurim*). And fifty days later, the outpouring of the Holy Spirit (Pentecost) happened at the Jewish Feast of Weeks (*Shavuot*). The connection between these pivotal New Testament events and the holy days appointed by God in the Torah can be no coincidence. As Dr. Moishe Rosen, a Jewish believer in Christ notes:

> As God ordered the universe and commanded the seasons of nature, He ordained times and seasons to usher in His plan of salvation for the human race. Israel's feasts of Jehovah portray stages of God's dealings with humanity, which culminate in the completion of the plan of salvation.[75]

Jesus' final meal before His crucifixion—the "Last Supper" as recorded in the Gospels[76] and mentioned in 1 Corinthians 11:17-34—

---

[75] Ceil Rosen and Moishe Rosen, *Christ in the Passover* (Chicago: Moody Publishers, 2006), p. 16.
[76] Matthew 26:17–30; Mark 14:12–26; Luke 22:7–39; John 13:1–17:26.

was a Passover Seder. And He partook of this meal with His Jewish disciples. The connection between Jesus and Passover was not lost on the Jewish New Testament authors. They openly referred to Christ as our Passover lamb.[77] Indeed, Luke began his narrative of the Last Supper with a bit of prescient foreshadowing. "Then came the day of Unleavened Bread, on which the Passover lamb had to be sacrificed" (Luke 22:7).

There is an additional fascinating point of connection between Christ and Passover in the wine served during the Seder. Dr. Rosen points out the significance of the third of the four cups of wine taken during the meal:

> [It] had two names: the "cup of blessing" because it came after the blessing or grace after meals, and the "cup of redemption" because it represented the blood of the Paschal lamb. It was of this cup that Jesus said, "This is my blood of the new testament [covenant]" (Matthew 26:28 KJV). It is *this* cup of blessing that Paul mentions in 1 Corinthians 10:16 . . . The death and resurrection of Jesus the Messiah are forever interwoven with the Passover and its symbolism. The Passover lamb spoke of the Lamb of God who was to come. The redemption from Egypt foreshadowed the greater redemption that Jesus would bring.[78]

We cannot deny the biblical link between Passover and Christ's sacrifice. In His sovereignty, God ordained the shedding of innocent blood as the means through which His people would find salvation from His judgment. "For the life of the flesh is in the blood . . . it is the blood that makes atonement by the life" (Lev 17:11). At the original

---

[77] John 1:29, 36; 1 Corinthians 5:7; 1 Peter 1:19; Revelation 5:6-8.
[78] Rosen & Rosen, 2006, pp. 70-71.

Passover, this played out in the tenth plague (Ex 12). The blood of the unblemished Passover lamb secured Israel's salvation and her freedom from slavery in Egypt. And when God gave Israel the Passover requirement, He knew that roughly 1,300 years later, a similar (though far more momentous) scenario would play out. Christ's innocent blood would be shed as the means through which God's people would find salvation from His judgment and secure their freedom from slavery to sin and death.

When Jesus broke the bread and drank the wine at the Last Supper, He was linking His imminent death to Passover. Both Passover and the Lord's Supper commemorate the shedding of innocent blood for salvation, leading to freedom for God's people. Because Passover was initially given in light of the future Messiah and His saving work on the cross, the original Passover becomes all the more poignant in Christ. At the same time, the inauguration of the New Covenant meant the Law of Moses—including the Pesach obligation—was fulfilled by Jesus and had become non-compulsory.[79] The original Passover pointed to Christ. Now that He has come, the Lord's Supper is the new Passover, elevated to a regular, even weekly, observance for God's people. Indeed,

> The Lord's Supper very quickly became a focal point of the early church's Sunday worship. As . . . the promise of Christ's presence in the worshipping fellowship, it was an obviously appropriate Christian way of celebrating the first day of the week.[80]

Easter, on the other hand, commemorates the Resurrection, a unique act of God in history. There are perhaps hints and shadows of the Resurrection in the Tanakh—the delivery of Noah's family from

---

[79] Galatians 3:23-29; Colossians 2:16-17; Hebrews 8:13.
[80] Barry et al., 2012, *Lord's Supper.*

the flood, the rescue of Joseph from the pit, Jonah's three days in a giant fish, God's provision of a substitute for Isaac's sacrifice. However, the substance behind those shadows, the real Resurrection, has no equivalent in history and no clear counterpart in the original Passover. The Resurrection was a divine, sovereign, unprecedented move of Yahweh. God incarnate "humbled himself by becoming obedient to the point of death, even death on a cross" (Phil 2:8). He died for our sins[81] once for all[82] and on the third day rose from the dead,[83] conquering death and sin.[84] The Resurrection validates the sacrifice. Without it, Christianity falls apart (1 Cor 15:14-18).

Remarkably, as significant as the Resurrection is, there is no command in Scripture to remember it or keep it holy. There are no New Testament commands for or against commemorating Christ's resurrection.[85] Indeed, Easter as a celebration or holy day does not appear in Scripture.[86] The Christian holiday of Easter was actually a later development of church tradition. And, interestingly, the New Testament acknowledges the validity of such manmade traditions that honor God. In John's gospel, the apostle mentions a minor detail that reveals something significant.

> At that time the Feast of Dedication took place at Jerusalem. It was winter, and Jesus was walking in the temple, in the colonnade of Solomon. (John 10:22-23)

---

[81] Romans 5:8; 2 Corinthians 5:21; Colossians 2:14; 1 Peter 2:24-25; 1 John 2:2.

[82] Hebrews 7:27, 10:10-12.

[83] Matthew 28:5-6; Mark 16:6; Luke 24:6-7; John 20:8-9.

[84] 1 Corinthians 15:24-26; 2 Timothy 1:10; Hebrews 2:14.

[85] It is natural for Christians to contemplate the Resurrection in the sacrament of the Lord's Supper. However, the text for that commandment only commends the remembering of Christ's death. More relevant, perhaps, is baptism, in which "just as Christ was raised from the dead by the glory of the Father, we too might walk in newness of life" (Rom 6:4). That said, baptism is an event that only need occur once in a believer's life.

[86] The King James Version of the Bible incorrectly uses the word "Easter" in place of "Passover" in Acts 12:4.

The *Feast of Dedication* was established in 164 BC to celebrate the purging of the temple after its pollution by King Antiochus Epiphanes in 167 BC. After Judas Maccabaeus had driven out the invaders, the altar was rebuilt, the temple cleansed, and a Feast of Dedication was inaugurated to celebrate the event. M. G. Easton reveals that:

> The feast lasted for eight days, beginning on the 25th of the month Chisleu (December) . . . It was an occasion of much rejoicing and festivity."[87]

This celebration later became known as the *Feast of Lights*, or *Hanukkah*. While the NT does not explicitly state it, Jesus, as a Jew at the temple in Jerusalem during the Feast of Dedication, would have undoubtedly participated in the tradition. Indeed, John's inclusion of that particular detail is taken by many as an indication that the Feast of Dedication was at least one of the reasons Jesus was in Jerusalem at that time. Thus, the New Testament reveals that Christ participated in manmade traditions not given by God in the Torah. This biblical precedent validates those Christians who choose to commemorate Jesus' resurrection via manmade traditions such as Easter.

In sum, we can capture the baseline New Testament teaching on Passover/Easter in the following three points:

1. Under the New Covenant, the Law of Moses—including the Passover obligation—was fulfilled by Jesus. The Lord's Supper is now our Passover. Thus;

2. The celebration of the Jewish Passover is allowed but not required of Christians.

---

[87] M. G. Easton, *Easton's Bible Dictionary* (New York: Harper & Brothers, 1893), p. 365.

3. The New Testament neither requires nor condemns the celebration of Christ's resurrection. But it does teach the validity of manmade traditions that honor God.

CHAPTER 3

Early Christian Writings

WITH THE NEW TESTAMENT BASELINE ESTABLISHED, we now turn to a survey of early Christian writings outside of the New Testament. There is a common misconception that these documents were sophomoric and primitive. Some assume the writings were composed by uneducated men who folded pagan ideas and myths into whatever Christian truths they may have learned along the way. While there may have been some early writings that fit that description, they do not survive today. The early Christian writings that have stood the test of time paint a completely different picture. There we find a humble and passionate people with an earnest desire to follow the teachings of Jesus. They knew their Scripture well. And that includes both the Jewish Scriptures and the new apostolic writings. I found myself both surprised and encouraged by the spiritual maturity and theological sophistication I found in these writings.

Our focus will be on the documents that speak directly to the relationship between Jews and Christians and are dated between AD 50 and the Council of Nicaea in AD 325. The earliest of these documents were written simultaneously with the New Testament books and circulated among the early churches. Some were even written by men who personally knew the apostles. Christianity was finding its way during this era, trying to work out Jesus' teachings and the paradigm-shattering New Covenant He had ushered in. The Church found itself fighting battles on multiple fronts: persecution from the outside and heresies from within. It will be helpful to begin by looking at the social and historical context of the culture in which Christianity emerged.

HISTORICAL CONTEXT

Before we dive into the early writings, let's take a step back. It will be helpful to briefly survey the events that led up to this period of history and the forces at play when these early documents were being composed. Doing so will provide us with an accurate historical context as we examine the early documents and the men that wrote them. Historian Henry Chadwick sets the stage for us. "The reconstruction of Israelite society after the catastrophe of the Babylonian deportation [597-538 BC] had been firmly based on the law of Moses."[1] With no new prophets declaring God's word, the Jews had become a people of the book. They turned to the study of God's written revelation: Scripture. The scribes and "lawyers" of the rabbinical schools began to supplement the Hebrew Scriptures with extra-biblical traditions.[2]

At the time of Jesus, the Jews lived in their homeland and had a temple in Jerusalem. They even had a ruling authority in the Great Sanhedrin, the supreme religious body in the Land of Israel. However, Israel was not operating as an autonomous nation. After their return from Babylon, the Jews continued under a theocratic government of priests until the Roman general Pompey conquered Palestine and took Jerusalem by force in 63 BC. Historians Schaff & Wace note that upon conquering Jerusalem:

[1] Henry Chadwick, *The Early Church* (London; New York: Penguin Books, 1993), p. 11.
[2] This extra-biblical tradition eventually led to the sharp debates we see between Jesus and Jewish religious leaders.

Pompey's curiosity led him to penetrate into the Holy of Holies.[3] He was much impressed, however, by its simplicity and went away without disturbing its treasures, wondering at a religion which had no visible God.[4]

In 37 BC, the Romans gave the Kingdom of Judea to Herod the Great. This marked the first time in history that Israel had ever been ruled by a non-Jew (foreign blood). In this historical event, many saw biblical prophecy coming to pass:

> The scepter will not depart from Judah
> or the staff from between his feet
> until he whose right it is comes
> and the obedience of the peoples belongs to him.
> (Genesis 49:10, CSB)

In other words, the arrival of the *Mashiach* was imminent. Schaff & Wace note,

> When the Kingdom of the Jews had devolved upon such a man the expectation of the nations was, according to prophecy, already at the door. For with him their princes and governors, who had ruled in regular succession from the time of Moses came to an end.[5]

The Romans ruled the Jewish homeland, and their presence was pervasive in both law and military force. However, Rome was not the only influence that impacted Christianity. Ferguson notes:

> Three concentric circles of influence circumscribed the world in which early Christianity began. From the outside

---

[3] The Holy of Holies is the innermost, sacred room of the Jewish temple where only the High Priest was allowed to go once per year.
[4] Philip Schaff and Henry Wace, eds., *A Select Library of Nicene and Post-Nicene Fathers of the Christian Church*, vol. 14 (1890; repr., Edinburgh: T & T Clark, 1997), Ch. VI, 3.
[5] Ibid., Ch. VI, 4.

moving in, these influences were the Roman, the Greek, and the Jewish. The pattern of growth in the early church was the reverse.[6]

The Greek influences of the era were evident in the intellectual sphere, especially philosophy, language, and literature. Greek philosophy provided the vocabulary and intellectual framework through which Christian theology was initially expressed. So the Jewish culture into which Jesus was born was heavily influenced by Hellenism and Roman rule.

At the time of Christ, Judaism was not a monolithic belief system. There were various sects—Pharisees, Sadducees, Essenes, Zealots—that were often in sharp disagreement with one another over substantial theological matters. The Christian faith grew out of this Hebrew culture. In fact, it was initially seen as just another Jewish sect (often referred to as the "Nazarenes"). This is understandable considering that Jesus was Jewish, as were His Apostles and the NT authors. Moreover, they were preaching Jesus as the Jewish Messiah promised in the Hebrew Bible.[7]

The rise of Christianity notably coincided with the fall of Israel. Three unsuccessful revolts dashed her hopes of an independent homeland. The first uprising occurred in AD 66–73 in Jerusalem, resulting in the destruction of the temple as predicted by Jesus.[8] Forty years later (AD 115-117), the Jews who had been displaced to Cypress and North East Africa rebelled. Fifteen years after that, the Bar Kokhba revolt broke out under the emperor Hadrian (AD 132-135). After the third insurgence was put down, Hadrian issued several proclamations

---

[6] Ferguson, 2013, p. 27.
[7] The Jewish title *Mashiach* means "anointed." The Greek translation of "anointed" is *Christ*. This title is ascribed to Jesus more than five hundred times in the New Testament.
[8] Matthew 24:1-2; Mark 13:1-2; Luke 21:5-6.

aimed at what he saw as the cause of the repeated rebellions: Jewish nationalism in Judea.[9]

THE PARTING OF THE WAYS

Noted historian Henry Chadwick records that in its earliest days,

> The Church was deeply conscious of its solidarity with Israel, and of the continuity of God's action in the past with his present activity in Jesus of Nazareth and in his followers.[10]

Ferguson notes:

> The God of the Jews was the God of the early Christians, and the central affirmations of the early church—Jesus as the Messiah, his resurrection from the dead, a new age of the forgiveness of sins, and the gift of the Holy Spirit— took their meaning from Jewish hopes, based on the interpretation of the scriptural prophets and stimulated by the later apocalyptic literature of the Jews.[11]

The claims of Jesus were at the core of the conflict between the early Christians and the Jews. Was He the Messiah or a false prophet? The discord began as just one more sectarian dispute within the Jewish community. Roman historian Suetonius reports that during the reign of Claudius (~AD 49), Jews were expelled from Rome because of agitation over "Chrestus," referring to Christ.[12] Claudius saw the issue as a Jewish intramural dispute. A scene in the book of Acts further

---

[9] Hanan Eshel, "The Bar Kochba Revolt, 132-135," *The Cambridge History of Judaism* Volume 4, The Late Roman-Rabbinic Period, no. (July 17, 2006): p. 105.
[10] Chadwick, 1993, p. 12
[11] Ferguson, 2013, p. 31.
[12] Suetonius, 2008, *Claudius* 25.4. See also Acts 18:2.

reveals that the Roman government did not distinguish Christianity from the legally recognized Jewish religion:

> But when Gallio was proconsul of Achaia, the Jews made a united attack on Paul and brought him before the tribunal, saying, "This man is persuading people to worship God contrary to the law." But when Paul was about to open his mouth, Gallio said to the Jews, "If it were a matter of wrongdoing or vicious crime, O Jews, I would have reason to accept your complaint. But since it is a matter of questions about words and names and your own law, see to it yourselves. I refuse to be a judge of these things." And he drove them from the tribunal. (Acts 18:12-16)

In Palestine, although persecuted by the Jews (1 Thes 2:14-16), Christians remained a group within Judaism for some time. In Judea, however, the Jewish Christians were harshly resisted by the Jewish religious leaders. To ensure the exclusion of Jewish Christ-followers from the synagogues, the rabbis introduced the *Birkat ha-minim,*[13] a "benediction against the heretics." Jewish scholar Alan Segal notes:

> [Jewish rabbi] Gamaliel (about AD 80-115) ordered Samuel the Small to compose a 'benediction' against the *minim.* This would have made participation in synagogue services impossible for anyone identifying himself as a *min.*[14]

The *Birkat ha-minim* is number twelve in the *Shemoneh Esreh* (eighteen benedictions) that make up the required daily prayer of

---

[13] In Hebrew, *min* means "from, out of" and commonly refers to heretics. *Minim* is the plural form.

[14] Alan F. Segal, *Two Powers in Heaven: The Significance of the Rabbinic Reports about Binitarianism, Ditheism and Dualism for the History of Early Christianity and Judaism* (1977; repr., Waco, TX: Baylor University Press, 2002), p. 6.

religious Jews.[15] There are several known versions of the benediction, but the wording of the extant early *siddurim* (ninth to twelfth centuries) is believed to resemble the original closely. It reads:

> *For the apostates let there be no hope.*
> *And let the arrogant government be speedily uprooted in*
> *our days.*
> *Let the noẓerim [Nazarenes] and the minim [heretics] be*
> *destroyed in a moment.*
> *And let them be blotted out of the Book of Life and not be*
> *inscribed together with the righteous.*
> *Blessed art thou, O Lord, who humblest the arrogant.*

The curse is believed to have been written with several groups in view: Jewish Christians (apostates), Christians (enemies of the Jews), the governments of the Christian world, and heretics in general. According to Jewish scholar Shaye Cohen:

> Since the [Jewish] Christians could not recite this benediction, and presumably would have been uncomfortable in the presence of those who did, the effect of the institution of this benediction was to expel Christians from the synagogues. Scholars found confirmation for this interpretation in John's references to the expulsion of Christians from synagogues (John 9:22; 12:42; 16:2) and in the assertions of various church fathers that the Jews curse Christ and/or Christians in their daily prayers.[16]

Meanwhile, Gentile believers, who felt no allegiance to Jewish heritage or tradition, were often unsympathetic toward the destruction

---

[15] Modern Jews rarely hear this benediction because, on the Sabbath and holidays, an alternative version is used which does not reference *minim* (Kimelman, 1981).

[16] Cohen, 2014, p. 225.

of the temple and the subsequent scattering of the Jewish people. Some Gentile Christians even regarded the destruction as God's judgment on the nation of Israel for the murder and rejection of Jesus undertaken by her leaders. Thus, as we will see below, many Gentile Christians came to regard Jews as heretics and deniers of Christ. The ante-Nicene writings of the Church fathers and the rabbis reveal that the theological clash between Jews and Christians was a two-way street. Cohen asks:

> What explains the striking overlap in heresiological[17] perspective between the rabbis and the fathers? The term *minim* has to be thrown into the heretical pot, and it's use compared in detail to *haretikoi*.[18] Could the Jewish treatment of Christians perhaps have led to a Christian devaluation of others as "heretics"?[19]

Another distinguished Jewish scholar, Daniel Boyarin, remarks,

> In the tannaitic period (roughly equivalent to the period of ante-Nicene Christianity), rabbinic texts project a nascent and budding heresiology, different in content (in some ways complementary in content) but strikingly similar in form to that of the second century Fathers. In their very efforts to define themselves and mark themselves off from each other, Christian writers of orthodoxy and the rabbis were evolving in important and strikingly parallel ways.[20]

Exactly when or how Jews and Christians parted ways is a matter of debate in scholarship. The fire in Rome in AD 64 seems to mark an

---

[17] *Heresiology* is the study of heresies.
[18] *Haretikoi* is a Greek word that means "causing division" and is used to refer to heretics. It is found in Titus 3:10.
[19] Shaye J. D. Cohen (1980), "A Virgin Defiled: Some Rabbinic and Christian Views on the Origins of Heresy," In *Union Seminary Quarterly Review* 36, no. 1: pp. 1-11.
[20] Daniel Boyarin, *Borderlines: The Partition of Judaeo-Christianity* (Philadelphia, PA: University of Pennsylvania Press, 2004), p. 5.

early milestone along the way. Following the fire, which destroyed much of the city, Ferguson reveals that,

> Nero (or his magistrate) charged and punished Christians for the fire. Tacitus, the Roman historian who reports the incident (*Annals* 15.44) did not give much credence to the charge of arson, but he did consider Christianity a "deadly superstition" deserving punishment for "hatred of the human race."[21]

From then on, the authorities in Rome recognized Christians as distinct from Jews. However, a parting of the ways between the two religions would not occur until at least the second century. Basil Studer notes, "From the socio-political point of view, Christianity fairly soon broke away from Judaism. Already by about AD 130, the final break had been affected."[22] Scholar James D. G. Dunn agrees that following the Bar Kokhba revolt of AD 132-135, "the separation of the main bodies of Christianity and Judaism was clear-cut and final, whatever interaction there continued to be at the margins."[23] Yitzhaq Baer concurs: "With the Bar Kokhba rising, the final rift between Judaism and Christianity was complete."[24]

Boyarin, however, takes a slightly different view:

> In the earliest stages of their development—indeed I suggest until the end of the fourth century, if we consider all of their varieties and not just the nascent "orthodox" ones—Judaism and Christianity were phenomenologically indistinguishable as entities, not

---

[21] Ferguson, 2013, p. 66.

[22] Basil Studer and Andrew Louth (1992), *Trinity and Incarnation: The Faith of the Early Church* (Collegeville, Minn.: Liturgical Press), p. 14.

[23] James D G Dunn (1991), *The Partings of the Ways: Between Christianity and Judaism and Their Significance for the Character of Christianity* (London: Scm Press; Philadelphia), p. 135.

[24] Yitzhaq Baer (1961), "Israel, the Christian Church, and the Roman Empire from the Time of the Spetimius Severus to the Edict of Toleration of AD 313," *Studies in History*.

merely in the conventionally accepted sense, that Christianity was a Judaism, but also in the sense that differences that were in the fullness of time to constitute the very basis for the distinction between the "two religions" ran through and not between the nascent groups of Jesus-following Jews and Jews who did not follow Jesus.[25]

Cohen notes:

What did change after 70 CE was that Jews, or at least the rabbis, were no longer as eager to sell their spiritual wares to the Gentiles . . . Perhaps (and this is the common explanation) the rabbis saw the growing power of Christianity and decided not to try to compete with it. Outside of rabbinic circles, perhaps some Jews still actively tried to interest Gentiles, especially Christians, in Judaism, but the evidence for such activity is minimal.[26]

EARLY WRITINGS

Much is known about the first three hundred years of Christianity thanks to the prolific writings of the Apostolic and Church Fathers.[27] These writings tell of the founding of the Church's many congregations, the names of some of the earliest bishops and pastors, and even contain some of their sermons. They also record early hymns, prayers, responsive readings, doctrinal statements, and Bible commentary. Consequently, the modern understanding of early Christian history is remarkably detailed. Granted, some of these early

---

[25] Boyarin, 2004, pp. 89-90.
[26] Cohen, 2014, pp. 49-50.
[27] See Appendix C: List of Early Christian Writings Dated to the ante-Nicene Era.

writings were false gospels or scriptures. But, as Bennett notes, those writings,

> were condemned by the church as soon as they appeared. But this same church produced post-New Testament writings; works that, while not to be classified with the inerrant word of God, do accurately represent the character, teachings, and practices of the very earliest Christians . . . they have all the authority—not, indeed, of Scripture—but of history.[28]

It is important to remember that there was no "New Testament" during this era. Although all of the writings that would eventually comprise the New Testament were completed before AD 100, the official canon of New Testament books would not be finalized or published together for hundreds of years. Instead, the individual epistles and gospels of the New Testament were copied and distributed among Christian communities. Early Christians would, for example, read and share Paul's various letters, or the scroll called "Luke/Acts," which contained Luke's Gospel plus the Acts of the Apostles. And these biblical writings would be shared and even copied alongside extra-biblical writings of the time.

Space does not allow us a comprehensive review of the complete body of available early writings. But we will examine several major works that speak directly to our study of Jewish-Christian relations. We will begin our survey with what is undoubtedly the most anti-Jewish teaching of the period, *Marcionism*. Then we will look at the two works that Jewish scholar Shaye Cohen considers the foremost anti-Jewish texts of the second century: Justin Martyr's *Dialogue with Trypho* and Melito's *On the Pascha*. And lastly, we will examine

---

[28] Rod Bennett, *Four Witnesses: The Early Church in Her Own Words* (San Francisco: Ignatius Press, 2002), p. 10.

Cyprian's third-century work *Three Books of Testimonies Against the Jews*. These selected writings do not represent the views of every single Christian during these centuries, of course. But as enduring works from known authors, they provide a credible look at the attitudes and beliefs of Christendom at the time. This section will end with an examination of what the early Church writings have to say about our two markers: Sabbath/Lord's Day and Passover/Easter.

MARCIONISM

Marcion of Sinope (AD 85-160) is a historical figure who embodied the sort of potent anti-Jewish sentiment many believe was prevalent in the ante-Nicene era. A great deal is known about Marcion through early writings, making him an excellent case study for us. He taught that the Bible refers to two different gods; the benevolent God of love and mercy proclaimed by Jesus and the "finite, imperfect, angry Jehovah of the Jews." In his work *Antitheses* (AD 144), Marcion outlined this contrast, describing the God of the Old Testament as a *demiurge*—a lesser god who created the physical universe. He considered this deity a harsh Jewish tribal god, as severe and unmerciful as his law. The Old Testament God commanded us to love our neighbor but hate our enemies. He taught vengeance, saying, "An eye for an eye, and a tooth for a tooth." By contrast, Marcion argued, the Supreme God of the New Testament commands us to love our enemy and "turn the other cheek."

Marcion believed the creator god of the Hebrew Bible was righteous and just in the sense of administering justice—giving men what they merited based on their actions. However, this god was not the father of Jesus. Rather, Christ descended from a previously unknown God of the New Testament. Marcion taught that Jesus materialized in human form at the start of His mission as a messenger of this "good God." The Old Testament god created the universe; the

New Testament God was the author of salvation. Because of the stark contrast Marcion saw between the Old and New Testaments, he concluded Christianity was wholly disconnected from Judaism. Thus, he could only accept those parts of Scripture that corroborated his theology. Ferguson notes,

> [Marcion] rejected the Old Testament as scripture for the church and issued a New Testament consisting of edited versions of the Gospel of Luke and ten Pauline epistles (lacking the pastoral epistles). He omitted or changed verses, often on a dogmatic basis.[29]

Specifically, Marcion edited Luke to remove any mention of the Incarnation. He also amended Paul's letters to avoid the notion that Jesus fulfilled the prophecies of the Hebrew Scriptures or participated in the work of creation. Because his superior New Testament god was previously unknown, Marcion rejected the Jewish Bible as unconnected to salvation. And since Christ was utterly unknown until He appeared, the Tanakh did not contain any actual prophecies of the true Messiah. Segal notes that "Marcion felt that the Jewish Messiah, as a representative of the just God, was prophesied and would appear as a kind of anti-Christ."[30]

The Church fathers met Marcion's anti-Jewish theology with ferocious opposition, rejecting it outright as heresy. They wanted nothing to do with his divisive teachings, and Marcion was excommunicated from the Church. The rejection of Marcion's heresy underscored early Christianity's "realization that it could not surrender its Old Testament roots and what that entailed about the oneness of God and the goodness of his creation."[31] Segal points out that Marcion's "canon of New Testament writings was dangerous, and the

---

[29] Ferguson, 2013, p. 87.
[30] Segal, 2002, p. 237.
[31] Ferguson, 2013, p. 89.

church required the Old Testament authority in order to foretell the coming of the Christian Messiah."[32] Ferguson tells us that Marcion was quite wealthy, and earlier in his career he,

> went to Rome and gave the church a large sum of money. His teachings, however, were rejected in 144, and his money was returned to him. He proceeded to set up a rival church that in a few years was nearly as widespread as the great church.[33]

Marcion used his personal wealth (including the returned donation) to fund a new ecclesiastical movement. Consequently, his heresy lingered in one form or another for at least three centuries after his death in AD 160 before finally fading into obscurity.[34] During that period, Marcion's teachings were written against at great length. Most notable was Tertullian's five-book commentary *Adversus Marcionem* (Against Marcion), published around AD 208. A century later, the Roman emperor Constantine ordered the Marcionite's meeting-houses handed over to the Church. He further banned the Marcionites from worshipping in public or private. The Church fathers agreed Marcion's teachings should be allowed no place in Christian doctrine. It was their urgent desire to respond to Marcion's heretical claims and to set the record straight before his anti-Jewish heresy spread further that hastened the establishment of the Christian biblical canon.

An additional element of Marcion's story is relevant to the relationship between Judaism and Christianity during this period. Tradition holds that Marcion asked Polycarp for recognition as bishop

---

[32] Segal, 2002, p. 236.
[33] Ferguson, 2013, p. 87.
[34] Nikolai Berdyaev, "Marcionism," www.berdyaev.com, 1928, www.berdyaev.com/berdiaev/berd_lib/1928_336.html.

only to be rejected with the words, "I recognize you...as the firstborn of Satan!" Segal notes:

> The term "firstborn of Satan" has a Hebrew equivalent which seems to have had a similar and contemporary use within Jewish exegesis as a term of reproach for someone who did not follow the accepted tradition of scriptural interpretation . . . such common terminology between Jewish and Christian communities is important to us because it points to a relationship between them.[35]

Indeed, Marcion's teachings represented as much a threat to Christianity as to Judaism. Segal continues:

> If the rabbis were concerned with Marcionite theology, they might have been dependent on the church fathers for their defense against him. It is also possible that each community developed its defense against Marcion independently.[36]

Segal further demonstrates that Tertullian relied on rabbinic tradition directly or indirectly through other church fathers who had used it in their battles with heretics.[37] At the same time, Tertullian used his refutation of Marcion as an occasion to also rebuke the anti-Christian teachings of Judaism: "It is now possible for the heretic to learn, and the Jew as well, what he ought to know already, the reason for the Jews errors."[38] He further wrote:

> Let the heretic now give up borrowing poison from the Jew—the asp as they say, from the viper: let him from now

---

[35] Segal, 2002, pp. 234-235.
[36] Segal, 2002, p. 236.
[37] Segal, 2002, pp. 241-242.
[38] Tertullian. (1972). *Adversus Marcionem* (E. Evans, Trans.). Oxford University Press. (Original work published ca. AD 208), III, 7.

on belch forth the slime of his own particular devices, as he maintains that Christ was a phantasm: except that this opinion too will have had other inventors, those so to speak premature and abortive Marcionites whom the apostle John pronounced antichrist, who denied that Christ was come in the flesh.[39]

Tertullian's true adversary was any belief system—Marcionism, Judaism, or any other *ism*—that sought to deny Christ. It is in this sense that the Marcionite controversy served as a galvanizing force in early Christianity. Such is the benefit of heretical claims when rightly received. They obligate believers to re-examine their Scriptural understandings and either reaffirm or adjust them as appropriate. This was the case with Marcion. Theologian Augustus Strong notes:

> If Marcion's view had prevailed, the Old Testament would have been lost to the Christian Church. God's revelation would have been deprived of its proof from prophecy. Development from the past, and divine conduct of Jewish history would have been denied . . . the love and mercy revealed in the New Testament would seem characteristic of a weak being, who could not enforce law or inspire respect. A tree has as much breadth below ground as there is above; so the OT roots of God's revelation are as extensive and necessary as are its NT trunk and branches and leaves.[40]

---

[39] Ibid., III, 8.
[40] Augustus Hopkins Strong (2009), *Systematic Theology: A Compendium Designed for the Use of Theological Students* (Valley Forge, Pa: Judson Press), p. 273.

DIALOGUE WITH TRYPHO

Christianity has always had an inherent tension in its relationship with Judaism. On the one hand, Christianity depends on the authority of the Hebrew Bible—and the Jewish testimony to those texts—to authenticate the New Testament and its claims about Christ. Yet, on the other hand, Christianity's claims to fulfill the Jewish prophecies involve a rejection of Judaism for its failure to acknowledge Jesus as the Messiah. There is perhaps no ancient writing in which this tension is more evident than Justin Martyr's *Dialogue with Trypho* (~AD 160).

Born in the Roman colony of Neapolis in Samaria (he was neither a Samaritan nor a Jew), Justin Martyr was arguably the most influential Christian apologist of the second century. *Dialogue with Trypho* is an intellectually impressive and lengthy document. (The English translation runs more than 69,000 words.) Justin writes with three principal issues in view: the purpose and meaning of the Law (Torah), the messianic claims about Jesus, and the identification of the true people of God. He works through these issues by way of an ambitious dialogue between himself and a Hellenized rabbi named Trypho, famous as one of the most learned Jews in the East. Whether this work records an actual discussion is a matter of debate. However, Justin's remarkable knowledge of the Jews, their objections to Christianity, and their Scripture suggest the content of *Dialogue* is based on actual conversations with Jews.

Justin argues from the truths of the Hebrew scriptures to their fulfillment in Christ in a work that Ferguson calls "the fullest statement from the early church of its arguments with Judaism."[41] *Dialogue* gives us a telling glimpse into the state of Christianity in the second century as it was finding its way and trying to work out what the New Covenant entailed. And that wasn't always easy to do so. For example, the

[41] Ferguson, 2013, p. 74.

document shows that Jewish followers of Christ were still a force in the mid-second century, and Justin considered them free to keep the Law of Moses. He felt Gentile Christians should be free to observe Jewish customs as well. However, he emphasized that such observances must be acknowledged as personal matters of conscience or preference, not requirements of salvation. Justin further revealed that many of his fellow Gentile Christians did not take so generous a view. Some held that those who kept the Mosaic Law could not be saved. Moreover, some Jewish followers of Christ demanded Gentiles keep the Law while others did not. Likewise, on the part of Gentile Christians. Some insisted Jewish believers give up the Law. Others (while denying the Law for Gentiles) allowed Jewish Christians to keep it.

It will be helpful to review a few excerpts from *Dialogue with Trypho* to appreciate both the tone and the nature of the discussion. This conversation happened very early in Christianity, within about 60 years of the apostle John's death. I found it fascinating to eavesdrop on a conversation between a Jewish rabbi and an early Christian from this era. Let's begin in chapter VII where the rabbi Trypho tells Justin:

> If, then, you are willing to listen to me (for I have already considered you a friend), first be circumcised, then observe what ordinances have been enacted with respect to the Sabbath, and the feasts, and the new moons of God; and, in a word, do all things which have been written in the law: and then perhaps you shall obtain mercy from God. But Christ—if He has indeed been born, and exists anywhere—is unknown, and does not even know Himself, and has no power until Elias come to anoint Him, and make Him manifest to all. And you, having accepted a

groundless report, invent a Christ for yourselves, and for his sake are inconsiderately perishing.[42]

In response, Justin underscores the continuity between Judaism and Christianity, pointing out they both worship one and the same God:

> There will be no other God, O Trypho, nor was there from eternity any other existing but He who made and disposed all this universe. Nor do we think that there is one God for us, another for you, but that He alone is God who led your fathers out from Egypt with a strong hand and a high arm. Nor have we trusted in any other (for there is no other), but in Him in whom you also have trusted, the God of Abraham, and of Isaac, and of Jacob.[43]

Justin then illuminates the differences between Jews and Christians and the nature of the new covenant:

> But we do not trust through Moses or through the law; for then we would do the same as yourselves . . . If, therefore, God proclaimed a new covenant which was to be instituted, and this for a light of the nations, we see and are persuaded that men approach God, leaving their idols and other unrighteousness, through the name of Him who was crucified, Jesus Christ . . . Moreover, by the works and by the attendant miracles, it is possible for all to understand that He is the new law, and the new covenant, and the expectation of those who out of every people wait for the good things of God.[44]

---

[42] Justin Martyr (1885). *Dialogue with Trypho* (A. Roberts, J. Donaldson, Eds., G. Reith, Trans.). T & T Clark. (Original work published ca. AD 160), VIII.
[43] Ibid., XI.
[44] Ibid., XI.

Notably, Justin does not portray the Jews as cut-off forever or rejected by God. Rather he indicates salvation in Jesus is available to the Jews. He goes on to identify where he believes the Jews went wrong:

> Accordingly, these things have happened to you in fairness and justice, for you have slain the Just One, and His prophets before Him; and now you reject those who hope in Him, and in Him who sent Him—God the Almighty and Maker of all things—cursing in your synagogues those that believe on Christ. For you have not the power to lay hands upon us, on account of those who now have the mastery. But as often as you could, you did so.[45] . . . For after that you had crucified Him . . . when you knew that He had risen from the dead and ascended to heaven . . . you not only did not repent of the wickedness which you had committed, but at that time you selected and sent out from Jerusalem chosen men through all the land to tell that the godless heresy of the Christians had sprung up, and to publish those things which all they who knew us not speak against us. So that you are the cause not only of your own unrighteousness, but in fact of that of all other men.[46]

The case Justin makes is strong and critical, to be sure. But it does have biblical grounds. His accusation that the unbelieving Jews are culpable in the death of Christ finds precedent in Peter's Pentecost sermon recorded in Acts 2:14-41. There the apostle indicted his Jewish audience by claiming they "crucified and killed [Jesus] by the hands of lawless men" (Acts 2:23b), even though most of the Jews he was

---

[45] Ibid., XVI.
[46] Ibid., XVII.

speaking to were not directly involved in Jesus' trial and execution. Likewise, Justin's scolding of Trypho and the Jews for denying Christ echoes the strong NT warnings we looked at earlier.[47]

In this passage, Justin also reveals that the Jews of his day were cursing and even laying hands on Christians for their faith in Christ. Fascinatingly, Jewish scholar Shaye Cohen notes:

> There is remarkable confluence between the Jewish view of Jesus in this passage and the Jewish view of Jesus in b. Sanhedrin 43a,[48] which also sees Jesus as an idolater and deceiver and which also attributes his execution to Jewish authorities acting without any involvement of the Romans.[49]

The careful reader will have noticed in Justin's comments several likely references to the Jewish *Birkat ha-minim* we looked at earlier.[50] Indeed, theologian W. Horbury notes:

> Trypho and his companions are told seven times in Justin's *Dialogue* . . . that 'you,' the Jews, curse believers in Christ . . . it is noted that this happens 'in your synagogues'."[51]

Trypho provides further insight into the Jewish attitude towards Christians at the time:

> And Trypho said, "Sir, it was good for us if we obeyed our teachers, who laid down a law that we should have no intercourse with any of you, and that we should not have

---

[47] Namely Matthew 10:32-33, Mark 8:38, 2 Peter 2:1-2, among others. See pages 31-32.

[48] This is a passage in the *Talmud*, the central text of Rabbinic Judaism and the primary source of Jewish religious law (halakha) and Jewish theology.

[49] Cohen, 2014, p. 240.

[50] See pages 58-59.

[51] W. Horbury, "The Benediction of the Minim and Early Jewish-Christian Controversy," *The Journal of Theological Studies* XXXIII, no. 1 (April 1, 1982): 19–61, https://doi.org/10.1093/jts/xxxiii.1.19.

even any communication with you on these questions. For you utter many blasphemies, in that you seek to persuade us that this crucified man was with Moses and Aaron, and spoke to them in the pillar of the cloud; then that he became man, was crucified, and ascended up to heaven, and comes again to earth, and ought to be worshipped."[52]

Justin responds:

Now it is not surprising that you hate us who hold these opinions and convict you of a continual hardness of heart. For indeed Elijah, conversing with God concerning you, speaks thus: "Lord, they have slain Thy prophets, and digged down Thine altars: and I am left alone, and they seek my life." And He answers him: "I have still seven thousand men who have not bowed the knee to Baal." Therefore, just as God did not inflict His anger on account of those seven thousand men, even so He has now neither yet inflicted judgment, nor does inflict it, knowing that daily some [of you] are becoming disciples in the name of Christ, and quitting the path of error; who are also receiving gifts, each as he is worthy, illumined through the name of this Christ.[53]

Justin's comments remind us of our earlier examination of Romans 9-11.[54] This is where Paul speaks of Israel's hardening and the remnant that will one day come to faith.

The apologist continues, assuring Trypho,

We do not hate you [Jews] or those who, by your means, have conceived such prejudices against us; but we pray

---

[52] Justin Martyr, ca. AD 160/1885, XXXVIII.
[53] Ibid., XXXIX.
[54] This was examined in Section 2: New Testament Writings, starting on page 15.

76

that even now all of you may repent and obtain mercy from God, the compassionate and long-suffering Father of all.[55]

Indeed, Justin earnestly desires that the Jews would come to salvation in Christ:

> Say no evil thing, my brothers, against Him that was crucified, and treat not scornfully the stripes wherewith all may be healed, even as we are healed. For it will be well if, persuaded by the Scriptures, you are circumcised from hard-heartedness . . . assent, therefore, and pour no ridicule on the Son of God; obey not the Pharisaic teachers, and scoff not at the King of Israel, as the rulers of your synagogues teach you to do after your prayers: for if he that touches those who are not pleasing to God, is as one that touches the apple of God's eye, how much more so is he that touches His beloved! And that this is He, has been sufficiently demonstrated.[56]

Dialogue with Trypho closes with Justin describing an amicable parting of the ways between the two men.

> After this they left me, wishing me safety in my voyage, and from every misfortune. And I, praying for them, said, "I can wish no better thing for you, sirs, than this, that, recognizing in this way that intelligence is given to every man, you may be of the same opinion as ourselves, and believe that Jesus is the Christ of God."[57]

---

[55] Ibid., CVII.
[56] Ibid., CXXXVII.
[57] Ibid., CLXII.

Summary of *Dialogue with Trypho*

In this early writing, Justin uses his remarkable command of Jewish Scripture to develop a forceful theological case for Christ. He also openly challenges the tenets of Judaism that reject Jesus. Notably, while mounting his argument, Justin makes no effort to distance Christianity from its Jewish roots. On the contrary, the apologist approaches the Hebrew Bible with reverence, speaking highly of the Jewish prophets and patriarchs and drawing numerous bold lines of connection between the Jewish Scriptures and Christ.

Whether or not this work records an actual conversation, what Justin wants his reader to take away is not hatred or persecution of the Jews. Instead, he models a biblical posture in which love and truth are held in balance. His tone is not disparaging, and he does not engage in personal attacks. At the same time, Justin pulls no punches when it comes to defending the truth of the New Testament and the person of Christ. *Dialogue with Trypho* is in many ways an ideal example of a respectful and honest debate in which Christianity is defended alongside an earnest desire for the salvation of the Jewish people.

ON THE PASCHA

Melito of Sarde's *On the Pascha* (~AD 170) was written around the same time as Justin's *Dialogue*. However, it is a lesser-known work and an entirely different sort of literature. The writing is believed to be a sermon intended for a Christian audience during the Paschal (Passover/Easter) season. As a *Quartodeciman*,[58] Melito would have celebrated the Resurrection on the Jewish date of 14 Nisan, concurrent with the Jewish Passover, rather than on the Sunday after the Paschal moon as most Christians had begun doing. In *On the Pascha*,[59] Melito

---

[58] The term comes from the Latin *quartus decimus*, which means "fourteenth."
[59] To read the sermon in its entirety, see Appendix D: On the Pascha.

recounts the Easter story by picking up the idea introduced by Paul (1 Cor 5:7) and John (John 1:29, 36) that Jesus was the unblemished Passover Lamb whose sacrifice brought forgiveness and salvation to His people.

The work is an examination of the mystery of the Passover, as Melito explains in his introduction:

> *Therefore, understand this, O beloved:*
> *The mystery of the Passover is new and old,*
> *eternal and temporal,*
> *corruptible and incorruptible,*
> *mortal and immortal in this fashion:*
> *It is old insofar as it concerns the law,*
> *but new insofar as it concerns the gospel;*
> *temporal insofar as it concerns the type,*
> *eternal because of grace;*
> *corruptible because of the sacrifice of the sheep,*
> *incorruptible because of the life of the Lord;*
> *mortal because of his burial in the earth,*
> *immortal because of his resurrection from the dead.[60]*

Melito begins his consideration of this mystery with a thorough, biblically-faithful survey of the Passover which God used to bring Israel out of slavery in Egypt.[61] He then connects the Passover to the person and work of Christ. In section II, Melito examines Israel's role in the death of Christ. Shaye Cohen gives us a Jewish perspective:

> For Melito, Christ the slaughtered Paschal lamb is also God and Lord. Melito draws the logical conclusion: the Jews (whom Melito calls "Israel") have murdered God,

---

[60] Melito, *On the Pascha*, in *Melito of Sardis on Pascha and Fragments*, trans. Stuart George Hall (Oxford: Clarendon, 1979). (Original work published ca. AD 170), 2-3.
[61] See Exodus 12.

with the result that Israel itself now "lies dead," rejected by God.[62]

The passage from *On the Pascha* that Cohen seems to be referring to is:

> Why was it like this, O Israel? You did not tremble for the Lord. You did not fear for the Lord. You did not lament for the Lord, yet you lamented for your firstborn. You did not tear your garments at the crucifixion of the Lord, yet you tore your garments for your own who were murdered. You forsook the Lord; you were not found by him. You dashed the Lord to the ground; you, too, were dashed to the ground, and lie quite dead.[63]

Just who does Melito have in mind when he refers to "Israel?" As a Quartodeciman who honored the Jewish calendar, it is hard to imagine Melito would be promoting anti-Jewishness. Indeed, Dr. Todd Hanneken finds Melito,

> closer to the Prophets and Sages than modern anti-Judaism. Melito identifies himself within the same tradition as those he criticizes, and he calls them to repentance with compassion.[64]

Cohen disagrees:

> Even though, or perhaps because, the practice of the Quartodecimans is close to Jewish usage, they were hardly close to Jews or Judaism, as Melito's invective shows.[65]

---

[62] Cohen, 2014, p. 237.
[63] Melito, ca. AD 170/1979, 99.
[64] Todd Russell Hanneken, "A Completely Different Reading of Melito's Peri Pascha," *Meqorot: The University of Chicago Journal of Jewish Studies*, no. 3 (1997): pp. 26-33.
[65] Cohen, 2014, p. 238.

Here, a brief note on what constitutes an anti-Jewish position is in order. Considered from the perspective of Jews who view the Jewish faith as integral to their very identity, it is entirely understandable they would feel personally offended or even attacked when their theology is challenged. And it must be granted that, throughout history, some Christians have treated some Jews horribly. The oppression and persecution of Jews—or any other people—must be categorically denounced as wrong and un-Christian. Jesus calls us to love our enemies and pray for those who persecute us. How much more should we love and serve our Jewish brothers and sisters!

As established in our New Testament baseline, Christians should not be opposed to the Jewish people. Instead, we are to recognize their central role in God's story and earnestly desire their salvation. At the same time, Christ-followers must reject any theology that denies Christ. This is a hard teaching for some to stomach. It can fly in the face of modern views of tolerance and inclusion. Yet, this is the position required of us by Jesus Himself. And it is why, from a Christian perspective, rejecting Judaism's denial of Christ and urging our Jewish brothers and sisters to repent and place their faith in Jesus is actually *pro-Jewish*. It honors the true Hebrew roots of the Christian faith and flows from a desire for the enteral salvation of the Jewish people.

Returning to Melito, what should we make of the line where the author tells Israel, "you, too, were dashed to the ground, and lie quite dead"? Again, as a keeper of the Jewish calendar (at least regarding Passover), Melito is not likely suggesting all Jews are dead. He may be hinting at a link between the Jewish leader's forsaking of Christ and the scattering of their nation in AD 70. However, based on the text that follows, the author's proclamation that Israel now lies "quite dead" is more likely a reference to unbelieving Jews being dead in their sin because they have rejected Christ. This brings to mind the words of Jesus:

> Therefore, I tell you, the kingdom of God will be taken away from you and given to a people producing its fruits. And the one who falls on this stone[66] will be broken to pieces; and when it falls on anyone, it will crush him. (Matthew 21:43-44)

Melito closes *On the Pascha* by declaring the final triumph of Christ who "gave the dead man life" by bringing forgiveness and salvation to all the families of the earth. We can reasonably assume his use of the universal term "all" includes Jews. Melito writes that Jesus,

> rose up from the dead, and cried aloud with this voice: Who is he who contends with me? Let him stand in opposition to me. I set the condemned man free; I gave the dead man life; I raised up the one who had been entombed . . . Therefore, come, all families of men, you who have been befouled with sins, and receive forgiveness for your sins. I am your forgiveness, I am the Passover of your salvation, I am the lamb which was sacrificed for you, I am your ransom, I am your light, I am your savior, I am your resurrection, I am your king, I am leading you up to the heights of heaven, I will show you the eternal Father, I will raise you up by my right hand.[67]

Summary of *On the Pascha*

In this Easter sermon, Melito offers a biblically-faithful retelling of the Passover and ties it to Christ's sacrifice as "the Lamb of God,

---

[66] Jesus is referring to Himself as "the stone that the builders rejected." See Matthew 21:42.
[67] Melito, ca. AD 170/1979, 101, 103. Emphasis added.

who takes away the sin of the world" (John 1:29). While his description of Israel's role in the death of Jesus may be seen as offensive from a Jewish perspective, it is not unbiblical. I did not find Melito's prose any more "anti-Jewish" than the New Testament, which, as we established earlier, is a collection of documents written to Jews by Jews about the Jewish Messiah. If you want to read his sermon for yourself and come to your own conclusion, you'll find it in its entirety at the end of this book (see Appendix D).

THREE BOOKS OF TESTIMONIES AGAINST THE JEWS

Cyprian (AD 210-285) was born in North Africa, became a bishop in AD 249, and remained a controversial figure during his lifetime. Known for his exceptional pastoral skills and accomplished Latin rhetoric, he was considered one of the foremost Latin writers of Western Christianity.[68] Among his many writings, Cyprian authored a treatise dated around AD 250 called *To Quirinius: Testimonies against the Jews*, which he delivered in three books. Scholar Claudio Moreschini explains that the work "was requested by a friend who wanted a compendium of the church's teaching on Judaism and on the relationship and opposition between Judaism and Christianity."[69] These writings from Cyprian give us a glimpse into the nature of Jewish-Christian relations a century after Justin and Melito.

---

[68] Henry Palmer Chapman, "St. Cyprian of Carthage," in *Catholic Encyclopedia*, ed. Charles Herbermann (New York: Robert Appleton Company, 1908), p. 694.
[69] Claudio Moreschini and Enrico Norelli (2005), *Early Christian Greek and Latin Literature: A Literary History from the Council of Nicea to the Beginning of the Medieval Period*, vol. 2 (Peabody, Mass.: Hendrickson Publishers), p. 366.

In Book I, Cyprian makes copious use of texts from the Old and New Testaments to lay out his case.[70] We can gather the nature and flow of his argument by simply reading through the section heads:

1. That the Jews have fallen under the heavy wrath of God, because they have departed from the Lord, and have followed idols.

2. Also because they did not believe the prophets, and put them to death.

3. That it was previously foretold that they would neither know the Lord, nor understand nor receive Him.

4. That the Jews would not understand the Holy Scriptures, but that they would be intelligible in the last times, after Christ had come.

5. That the Jews could understand nothing of the Scriptures unless they first believed on Christ.

6. That they would lose Jerusalem, and leave the land which they had received.

7. That they would also lose the Light of the Lord.

8. That the first circumcision of the flesh was made void, and a second circumcision of the spirit was promised instead.

9. That the former law, given by Moses, was about to cease.

10. That a new law was to be given.

11. That another dispensation and a new covenant was to be given.

12. That the old baptism was to cease, and a new one was to begin.

13. That the old yoke was to be made void, and a new yoke was to be given.

14. That the old pastors were to cease, and new ones to begin.

---

[70] Schaff adds a footnote I wholeheartedly agree with: "I cannot but note repeatedly how absolutely the primitive Fathers relied on the Holy Scriptures and commended a Berean use of them. Acts xvii." (Philip Schaff (1885), *Fathers of the Third Century: Hippolytus, Cyprian, Caius, Novatian, Appendix*. (repr., Grand Rapids, MI: Christian Classics Ethereal Library, 2004), footnote on p. 887.)

15. That Christ should be God's house and temple, and that the old temple should pass away,

16. and a new one should begin.

17. That the old sacrifice should be made void, and a new one should be celebrated.

18. That the old priesthood should cease, and a new priest should come who should be forever.

19. That another prophet, such as Moses, was promised, to wit, who should give a new testament, and who was rather to be listened to.

20. That two peoples were foretold, the elder and the younger; that is, the ancient people of the Jews, and the new one which should be of us.

21. That the Church, which had previously been barren, should have more sons from among

22. the Gentiles than the synagogue had had before.

23. That the Gentiles should rather believe in Christ.

24. That the Jews should lose the bread and the cup of Christ, and all His grace; while we should receive them, and that the new name of Christians should be blessed in the earth.

25. That rather the Gentiles than the Jews should attain to the kingdom of heaven.

26. That by this alone the Jews could obtain pardon of their sins, if they wash away the blood of Christ slain in His baptism, and, passing over into the Church, should obey His precepts.[71]

For the most part, Cyprian's argument appears to follow the contours of our five-point biblical framework. He acknowledges Israel's central role in God's story, along with the failure of her leaders.

---

[71] Philip Schaff, *Fathers of the Third Century: Hippolytus, Cyprian, Caius, Novatian, Appendix.* (1885; repr., Grand Rapids, MI: Christian Classics Ethereal Library, 2004), pp. 887-888.

He rejects their denial of Christ and, in the end, holds out hope for their salvation. However, some of Cyprian's ideas appear troublesome.

For example, sections four and five suggest the Jews could not understand Scripture except through Christ. This premise may seem anti-Jewish at first glance but turns out to be well-supported in Scripture. Among other passages, Cyprian cites the apostle Paul's teaching to the church at Corinth concerning the Israelites:

> But their minds were hardened. For to this day, when they read the old covenant, that same veil remains unlifted, because only through Christ is it taken away. Yes, to this day whenever Moses is read a veil lies over their hearts. But when one turns to the Lord, the veil is removed. (2 Corinthians 3:14-16)

Section seven also seems troublesome at first glance. It is headlined, "That they would also lose the Light of the Lord." However, as we read through this section, we find Cyprian's argument is related to the denial of Christ. He cites the apostle John in support of this point:

> Whoever believes in him is not condemned, but whoever does not believe is condemned already, because he has not believed in the name of the only Son of God. And this is the judgment: the light has come into the world, and people loved the darkness rather than the light because their works were evil. (John 3:18-19)

It was common among early Christian thinkers to overreach in reading prophecy and allegory into Scripture, and Cyprian was no exception. Thus, we can challenge certain points he makes. For example, section twenty is headlined, "That two peoples were foretold, the elder and the younger; that is, the old people of the Jews, and the new one which should consist of us." Cyprian comes to this conclusion based in part on God's pronouncement to Rebekah,

> Two nations are in your womb, and two peoples from
> within you shall be divided; the one shall be stronger than
> the other, the older shall serve the younger. (Genesis
> 25:23)

Cyprian's conclusion that this passage is a prophecy about Jews
and Christians doesn't seem warranted in context. And in hindsight, it
does not hold true. Christians are not of a different lineage than Jews.
In fact, Christianity is not about who we came from, but rather Who
we believe in. Therefore, we should prefer the plain meaning of this
passage in Genesis. Namely, that Rebekah will have twins, and each
will be the progenitor of a nation. And further, that the Jewish family
line of Abraham will continue through Jacob (the younger brother)
rather than Esau.

Likewise, section twenty-five: "That rather the Gentiles than the
Jews should attain to the kingdom of heaven." In support of this point,
Cyprian simply cites the following passage:

> I tell you, many will come from east and west and recline
> at table with Abraham, Isaac, and Jacob in the kingdom of
> heaven, while the sons of the kingdom will be thrown into
> the outer darkness. In that place there will be weeping and
> gnashing of teeth. (Matthew 8:11-12)

Cyprian appears to interpret Christ's words in this passage in a
decidedly anti-Jewish manner. He appears to be suggesting that Jews
cannot be believers in Christ and, thus, cannot be saved. However, in
point twenty-six he provides clarity:

> That by this alone the Jews can receive pardon of their
> sins, if they wash away the blood of Christ slain, in His
> baptism, and, passing over into His Church, obey His
> precepts. (26)

In other words, salvation is available to the Jewish people through faith in Christ. Consequently, taken in context, section twenty-five is perhaps better interpreted to mean, "Believers in Christ will attain to the kingdom of heaven but not religious Jews who reject Christ." If that connotation is accepted, Cyprian's final two points in Book I have a biblical basis. They echo the words of Peter and John before the council in Jerusalem, "And there is salvation in no one else, for there is no other name under heaven given among men by which we must be saved" (Acts 4:12). And also the words of Jesus to his disciple Thomas, "No one comes to the Father except through me" (John 14:6b).

Book II of *Testimonies Against the Jews* does not actually discuss the Jews in much depth. It is essentially a detailed (and remarkably accurate) Christology, again supported by abundant amounts of Scripture. It reveals Jesus as divine and as the promised Jewish Messiah. The book further proclaims Christ as the only way to salvation and teaches He will one day come as a judge and a king to reign forever. That said, there are two sections in Book II that contain possible points of offense concerning Jews.

Section fourteen is headlined, "That He was the righteous One whom the Jews should put to death." Here Cyprian quotes from Isaiah 57:1-2, Exodus 23:7, and Matthew 27:3-4 (and the Apocryphal book Wisdom of Solomon 2:12-22) to argue that the Messiah's death at the hands of the Jews was foretold. I found Cyprian's cited passages debatable. However, his point is both valid and biblical. The assertion that Jesus was rejected by His own people is validated in Mark 6:1-6, Luke 4:28-30, and John 5:43. And the culpability of the Jews in His death is addressed in Matt 27:25, Luke 23:18, and Acts 2:14-36. Thus, Cyprian's claims were not in error, just poorly supported.

Section twenty is entitled, "That the Jews should fasten Him to the Cross." It is essentially a reiteration of section fourteen. Here Cyprian is not alleging the Jews physically fastened Christ to the cross, but rather that it was foretold they would be guilty of His death. He quotes Isaiah, Jeremiah, Deuteronomy, Psalms, Numbers, Habakkuk, and Zechariah to outline what he sees as a prophetic foretelling of the cross in the Hebrew Bible. He then closes this section by quoting Jesus:

> And as Moses lifted up the serpent in the wilderness, so must the Son of Man be lifted up, that whoever believes in him may have eternal life. (John 3:14-15)

Interestingly, Book III of *Testimonies Against the Jews* does not discuss the Jews at all. Cyprian describes the contents of this book as,

> a succinct course of sacred reading for the religious teaching of our school . . . certain precepts of the Lord, and divine teachings, which may be easy and useful to the readers, in that a few things digested into a short space are both quickly read through, and are frequently repeated.[72]

This third book contains one hundred twenty short passages of Scripture or teachings. For example: "On the benefit of good works and mercy," "That brethren ought to sustain one another," and "That evil is not to be returned for evil." None of these passages speak to Jewish-Christian relations.

SUMMARY OF EARLY CHRISTIAN WRITINGS

In the early writings, we find evidence of struggle on the part of both Jews and early Christians, each trying to work out the boundaries of their beliefs. For example, in the *Didache,* the primitive Christian community expressed a desire to pray differently than the Jews, preferring to use the Lord's Prayer from Matthew 6:9-13. And they specifically chose Wednesdays and Fridays to fast because the Jews

[72] Schaff, 1885/2004, p. 93

fasted on Mondays and Thursdays. Likewise, the Jews introduced the *Birkat ha-minim*, (benediction against heretics) to pressure Jewish Christians out of the synagogues.

On the whole, however, the early Christian writings we've examined line up well with our five-point biblical perspective:

NT Framework	Early Christian Writings
1. Recognize Israel's central role in God's story	The early Church Fathers displayed a thorough understanding of the Hebrew Scriptures and the role Israel played as the nation through which Christ came. They also universally view Jesus as the Jewish Mashiach foretold in the Tanakh. However, the recognition of Israel and the Jewish people as having a privileged position does not appear as strong. It was alluded to by Justin in the second century and less so by Cyprian in the third.
2. Acknowledge the failure of Jewish religious leadership	The early Christian writers unanimously acknowledged the failure of the Jewish religious leadership.
3. Reject Jewish teachings that deny Christ	The early Christian writers unanimously rejected those Jewish teachings that deny Christ.
4. Understand Israel's future salvation	The record stands mostly silent on this issue. It is not explicitly discussed in the early writings we reviewed.
5. Love and earnestly desire the salvation of Jews	Justin expresses this desire outright. And in Melito and Cyprian, the salvation of Jews, if not directly addressed, is at least affirmed as

> available. It is unanimously promoted as part of the Gospel desire that all should come to salvation in Christ.

THE TWO MARKERS

Sabbath/Lord's Day

The hints in the New Testament of believers gathering on the first day of the week are confirmed in one of Christianity's earliest known extra-biblical writings, *The Teaching of the Lord to the Gentiles, Through the Twelve Apostles* (AD 60-120). More commonly known as *The Didache*, this document reveals that early Christians gathered on the first day of the week and referred to it as *The Lord's Day*. Section fourteen of this document[73] begins with:

> And on the Lord's own day gather yourselves together and break bread and give thanks, first confessing your transgressions, that your sacrifice may be pure.[74]

Indeed, Sunday gatherings began early in Christianity and continued through the first three centuries of the faith. The reason for this universal adoption of the first day of the week is no mystery. Jesus' resurrection on a Sunday is by far the most critical fact in all of Christendom. The apostle Paul taught of its significance:

> And if Christ has not been raised, our preaching is useless and so is your faith. More than that, we are then found to be false witnesses about God, for we have testified about

---

[73] Some translations include a heading for this section: "Christian Assembly on the Lord's Day" (Roberts-Donaldson), "Of Sunday Worship" (Staniforth), "The Sunday worship" (Kirsopp Lake).
[74] Maxwell Staniforth, *Early Christian Writings: The Apostolic Fathers* (New York: Dorset Press, 1968), p. 234.

God that he raised Christ from the dead . . . And if Christ has not been raised, your faith is futile; you are still in your sins. Then those also who have fallen asleep in Christ are lost. If only for this life we have hope in Christ, we are of all people most to be pitied. (1 Corinthians 15:14, 17-19)

If all of Scripture points to Christ and all of His work was validated by His resurrection, it is no exaggeration to categorize the Resurrection as the single most important event in the history of the human race. It is more important than the weekly Sabbath by far. Scholar Andrew Lincoln explains that the resurrection of Jesus,

> provided the first Christians with all the justification they needed to transfer the permanent significance of the Sabbath from the seventh day to the first. Just like the Sabbath, the Lord's Day was kept as a day of worship (centered on God's acts of new creation and redemption in Jesus) and—whenever possible—as a day of rest. Separation of worship and rest would never have occurred to a first-century Jew (for whom Sabbath rest was worship).[75]

It makes sense, then, that the early church, believing the legal Sabbath commandment was no longer binding, and understanding the staggering importance of the Resurrection, would gather together on the first day of the week—the day Jesus rose from the dead—and call it The Lord's Day. This view of Sabbath and the Lord's Day is consistent with the two points established in our New Testament baseline:

---

[75] Andrew T. Lincoln, "Sabbath to Lord's Day: A Biblical and Theological Perspective." In D. A. Carson (Ed.), *From Sabbath to Lord's Day: a biblical, historical and theological investigation*. (Wipf and Stock Publishers, 1999), p. 401.

1. Keeping the Jewish observance of the Sabbath on the last day of the week is allowed but no longer required.
2. Gathering on the first day of the week is also allowed but not required.

Passover/Easter

In 1 Corinthians, the apostle Paul wrote:

> Cleanse out the old leaven that you may be a new lump, as you really are unleavened. For Christ, our Passover lamb, has been sacrificed. Let us, therefore, celebrate the festival, not with the old leaven, the leaven of malice and evil, but with the unleavened bread of sincerity and truth. (1 Corinthians 5:7b-8)

The majority of early Christians were Jewish and, no doubt inspired by Paul's words, began to celebrate His resurrection annually as part of the Passover holiday. Eusebius tells us the Jewish Christians in Jerusalem celebrated the Resurrection in this way under the first fifteen bishops, who were of Jewish descent.[76] Rosen & Rosen tell us,

> The bishops sent out Paschal epistles every year to notify the Christians when Passover would fall according to the Jewish lunar calendar.[77]

In the early decades of Christianity, a disparity developed that played a role in dividing the Eastern Church from the Western Church. When it came to the annual commemoration of the Resurrection, Jewish Christians, along with some Gentiles, followed the Jewish calendar. They celebrated Jesus' resurrection on the 14th day of the Jewish month of Nisan, amid Passover. (This was the actual date of

---

[76] Eusebius, *Eccles. Hist*, 5.23.
[77] Rosen & Rosen, 2006 p. 71.

Jesus' Last Supper.) Most Gentile Christians, on the other hand, felt no allegiance to a Jewish calendar. They preferred to commemorate the Resurrection on the first day of the week since Sunday was the day Jesus' tomb was discovered empty.

The earliest mention of Christians celebrating the Resurrection comes to us from the second-century writings of Justin and Tertullian. However, it is believed the observance had been occurring for some time prior. Many historians hold that the annual remembrance of the Resurrection dates back to the first century. There is evidence in the New Testament that the commemoration of (or at least a reflection on) the Resurrection occurred as often as weekly among early Christians. Believers had begun gathering on the first day of the week to "break bread," a phrase regularly used in the NT to refer to the Lord's Supper.

At that time, the Church was a loose network of congregations scattered across the eastern Roman empire that lacked a central authority. Each community, led by a local bishop,[78] was free to choose how (or if) they wanted to commemorate the Resurrection. Thus, some communities would celebrate the Resurrection on 14 Nisan (Quartodecimans), while others chose the Sunday after Passover. Over the course of the first few centuries, the disagreement on a proper date became a significant controversy. The fourth-century historian Eusebius wrote:

> A question of no small importance arose at [the time of Pope Victor I, around AD 190]. The dioceses of all Asia, according to an ancient tradition, held that the fourteenth day, on which day the Jews were commanded to sacrifice the lamb, should always be observed as the feast of the life-giving pasch, contending that the fast ought to end on

---

[78] Bishops in the early church were not the formal authorities we see today. Rather they were typically the more educated church members chosen from among the community to lead the congregation. They were considered "first among equals."

that day, whatever day of the week it might happen to be. However, it was not the custom of the churches in the rest of the world to end it at this point, as they observed the practice, which from Apostolic tradition has prevailed to the present time, of terminating the fast on no other day than on that of the Resurrection of our Savior.[79]

The Church was torn between commemorating the resurrection of Christ on the date of the Jewish Passover or the day His tomb was found empty. And it turns out that no matter which day they chose, the early Church fell safely into the three-point New Testament baseline we identified:

1. Under the New Covenant, the Law of Moses—including the Passover obligation—was fulfilled by Jesus. The Lord's Supper is now our Passover. Thus;

2. The celebration of the Jewish Passover is allowed but not required of Christians.

3. The New Testament neither requires nor condemns the celebration of Christ's resurrection. But it does teach the validity of manmade traditions that honor God.

The biblical freedom afforded to Christians on this issue accounts for the variation in how and when the early Church celebrated the Resurrection. It also allows for the variation still found in the Church today.[80] In the end, because Scripture offers no commands for or against commemorating the Resurrection, there can be no "right" or "wrong" day to celebrate it. In the same way that freedom in Christ has made keeping Passover optional, celebrating the Resurrection is also a valid option for Christians.

---

[79] Eusebius of Caesarea, *Church History*, V, xxiii.
[80] Eastern Christianity follows the Julian Calendar rather than the Gregorian calendar used by most countries today and, therefore, observes Easter on a different date.

CHAPTER 4

The Council of Nicaea

HAVING ESTABLISHED A NEW TESTAMENT BASELINE and compared it to the writings of the early church, let us now turn to the final leg of our study and consider the Council of Nicaea.

HISTORICAL BACKGROUND

In AD 325, the Roman emperor Constantine convened the first ecumenical (global) Church council in history. The gathering took place in ancient Nicaea[1] from May through August of that year. It was attended by over 300 bishops from across the empire. Christianity had become a legal religion just twelve years earlier, in AD 313, thanks to the Edict of Milan. Historian Bruce Shelley sets the scene:

> July 4, 325, was a memorable day. About 300 Christian bishops and deacons from the eastern half of the Roman Empire had come to Nicaea, a little town near the Bosporus Straits flowing between the Black Sea and the Mediterranean. In the conference hall where they waited was a table. On it lay an open copy of the Gospels. The emperor, Constantine the Great, entered the hall in his imperial, jewel-encrusted, multicolored brocades, but out of respect for the Christian leaders, without his customary

---

[1] Modern-day İznik, Turkey.

train of soldiers. Constantine spoke only briefly. He told the churchmen they had to come to some agreement on the crucial questions dividing them. "Division in the church," he said, "is worse than war." The bishops and deacons were deeply impressed. After three centuries of periodic persecutions instigated by some Roman emperor, were they actually gathered before one not as enemies but as allies? Some of them carried scars of the imperial lash. One pastor from Egypt was missing an eye; another was crippled in both hands as a result of red-hot irons. But Constantine had dropped the sword of persecution in order to take up the cross. Just before a decisive battle in 312, he had converted to Christianity.[2]

It is worth noting that, according to Schaff & Wace, the Church Fathers who met at this council,

> understood their position to be that of witnesses, not that of exegetes . . . the first requirement was not learning, but honesty. The question they were called upon to answer was not, "What do I think probable, or even certain, from Holy Scripture?" but, "What have I been taught, what has been entrusted to me to hand down to others?"[3]

The Church was not only finding its way ecclesiastically but theologically as well. Although a body of accepted writings enjoyed consensus at the time of Nicaea, the Church would not establish an official New Testament canon of books for many years. The Christian understanding of the Trinity was still in its infancy, as well.

---

[2] Bruce L. Shelley (1990), "325 the First Council of Nicea," In *Christian History (#28)*, www.christianhistoryinstitute.org/magazine/article/first-council-of-nicea.

[3] Philip Schaff and Henry Wace, eds., *A Select Library of Nicene and Post-Nicene Fathers of the Christian Church*, vol. 14 (1890; repr., Edinburgh: T & T Clark, 1997), p. 40.

Those who believe that racism in the early Church led to a corruption of Christian theology typically point to the Council of Nicaea as "ground zero." It is here, they claim, the anti-Semitic sentiments that grew among early Christian leaders solidified into an anti-Jewish doctrine agreed on by the whole Church. Nicaea, it is alleged, is where Christianity officially left the Torah behind. It is where Passover was exchanged for Easter, and the Saturday Sabbath was replaced with Sunday worship.

However, as we have seen, long before Nicaea, a pattern had organically emerged in the Church on many of these issues. And ironically, the Council of Nicaea did not discuss the Jewish Bible, nor (despite popular allegations) did they determine the NT canon, the doctrine of the Trinity, or discuss the Sabbath. The Council's primary task was addressing the Empire-wide uproar caused by the Arian controversy.[4] Their secondary accomplishment was establishing church-wide uniformity concerning bishops, church membership, and other ecclesiastical matters.[5]

THE CANONS AND THEOLOGY OF THE COUNCIL

With the young Christian Church spreading quickly across the empire, unity was foremost in the minds of Constantine and the bishops. Consequently, the Council of Nicaea issued twenty canons primarily concerned with church procedure and the uniformity of religious observances. The canons addressed issues such as how to appoint bishops, circumstances under which bishops can be deposed and restored, jurisdictional boundaries, church membership, and other logistical affairs. Our concern, however, is the theology of the council,

---

[4] *Arianism* was a heresy that taught Jesus, as the Son of God, was not co-eternal with God the Father. Instead, Jesus was an entity distinct from and subordinate to God.
[5] There is good reason to believe that the celibacy of the priesthood was introduced and rejected at the Council.

and we find that summarized in the official creed they composed. The original version of the Nicene Creed, published in AD 325,[6] reads:

> *We believe in one God, the Father almighty,*
> *maker of all things visible and invisible,*
> *and in one Lord, Jesus Christ, the Son of God,*
> *begotten from the Father, only-begotten, that is, from the*
> *substance of the Father.*
> *God from God, light from light,*
> *true God from true God, begotten not made,*
> *of one substance with the Father, through Whom all*
> *things came into being, things in heaven and things on*
> *earth,*
> *Who because of us men and because of our salvation,*
> *came down, and became incarnate and became man.*
> *He suffered and rose again on the third day,*
> *and ascended to the heavens,*
> *and will come to judge the living and dead.*
> *And [we believe] in the Holy Spirit.*
> *But as for those who say there was when He was not,*
> *and, before being born, He was not,*
> *and that He came into existence out of nothing,*
> *or who assert that the Son of God is of a different*
> *hypostasis or substance,*
> *or created, or is subject to alteration or change—*
> *these the apostolic and catholic Church anathematizes.*

This document contains no suggestion of anti-Jewish sentiment. In fact, in the only lines correlating to Judaism, the creed endorses the foundational Jewish teaching that there is only one God and it was

---

[6] The Church modified the creed in AD 381 at the Second Ecumenical Council held in Constantinople. That council added language about the Holy Spirit as worshipped and glorified along with the Father and the Son.

through Him that all things were created. Moreover, the bishops of the council universally considered the Jewish Bible part of Holy Scripture. The sacred text of the Jews was wholly accepted as a sacred text by Christians from the very beginning.

Regardless of whatever anti-Jewish biases may have existed among the members of this church council, the creed and the canons it generated for posterity are not anti-Jewish. In fact, other than Marcion, whose heresy was roundly rejected, there is little evidence to suggest the Church Fathers at any time in the ante-Nicene era—nor at the Council of Nicaea itself—sought to remove the "Jewishness" from Christian theology. Theologian Thomas Oden notes:

> Nicaea was a milestone not because it presented something new, but because it held to that same faith that had been received directly from the apostles through the Spirit and with minimal perversion.[7]

SUMMARY OF NICAEA

The primary achievement of the Council of Nicaea was settling the Arian controversy. They did so by condemning Arius as a heretic. The discussion that led to this pronouncement shows no evidence of anti-Jewish influence. In fact, the decision, given in the form of the Nicene Creed, relied directly on the Jewish Scriptures. In addition to this creed, the council issued twenty canons that were ecclesiastical rather than theological in nature. These, too, had no direct correlation to the Church's attitudes toward Jews or Judaism.

The artifacts and decisions generated by the Council of Nicaea reveal some variation from our five-point biblical baseline. There is

---

[7] Oden, T. C. (2011). "The Faith Once Delivered: Nicaea and Evangelic Confession". In T. George (Ed.), *Evangelicals and Nicene Faith: Reclaiming the Apostolic Witness*. (Baker Publishing Group), p. 39.

little in the recorded discussions at Nicaea that directly corresponds to our framework. However, we can glean insight on the prevailing theology of the time through contemporaneous writers such as Pamphilus of Caesarea, Peter of Alexandria, and Eusebius of Caesarea. Thus, we can reasonably conclude that the work of the council remained strong theologically. It is in the area of attitudes that we see a shift at Nicaea. Evidence of this comes in a letter written just after the council regarding the date for keeping Easter. We will look at this in detail below when we review our two theological markers.

NT Framework	Early Christian Writings
1. Recognize Israel's central role in God's story	There are no recorded discussions that directly reveal the council's position on these points. Based on the prevailing theology of the Church at the time, we may conclude the bishops implicitly recognized Israel's central role in God's story. In particular, they recognized Jesus as the Jewish Messiah of the Hebrew Bible. Likewise, they tacitly acknowledged the failure of Jewish religious leaders to recognize Him, and reject Jewish teachings that deny Christ.
2. Acknowledge the failure of Jewish religious leadership	
3. Reject Jewish teachings that deny Christ	
4. Understand Israel's future salvation	The record stands silent on this issue. It was not explicitly discussed.
5. Love and earnestly desire the salvation of Jews	Here we see a shift in attitude of the council—or, at least, of Constantine—to a more divisive, personal tone. See the section on Easter below.

THE TWO MARKERS

Sabbath/Lord's Day

The Council of Nicaea made no official declarations regarding Sabbath or the Lord's Day. There is no evidence to suggest it was even discussed. As we saw earlier, Christians had been regularly meeting on the first day of the week for nearly three hundred years before the council was convened. Consequently, gathering on the Lord's Day rather than the Sabbath was taken as normative by the time of Nicaea. For example, Nicene Canon XX reads:

> Forasmuch as there are certain persons who kneel on the Lord's Day and in the days of Pentecost, therefore, to the intent that all things may be uniformly observed everywhere (in every parish), it seems good to the holy Synod that prayer be made to God standing.

Passover/Easter

The outcome of the Council of Nicaea most pertinent to our study is its verdict on Easter. What was ultimately established was independence from the Jewish calendar for the sake of church-wide uniformity. Eusebius records a letter from Constantine to those not present at the council.[8] The opening paragraph of *On the Keeping of Easter* reads:

> When the question relative to the sacred festival of Easter arose, it was universally thought that it would be convenient that all should keep the feast on one day; for what could be more beautiful and more desirable than to see this festival, through which we receive the hope of

---

[8] See Appendix E: *On the Keeping of Easter* to read the letter in its entirety.

immortality, celebrated by all with one accord, and in the same manner? It was declared to be particularly unworthy for this, the holiest of all festivals, to follow the custom [the calculation] of the Jews, who had soiled their hands with the most fearful of crimes, and whose minds were blinded. In rejecting their custom, we may transmit to our descendants the legitimate mode of celebrating Easter, which we have observed from the time of the Savior's Passion to the present day [according to the day of the week]. We ought not, therefore, to have anything in common with the Jews, for the Savior has shown us another way; our worship follows a more legitimate and more convenient course (the order of the days of the week); and consequently, in unanimously adopting this mode, we desire, dearest brethren, to separate ourselves from the detestable company of the Jews, for it is truly shameful for us to hear them boast that without their direction we could not keep this feast.[9]

Keeping in mind the difficulty our modern minds have not seeing race as a motivation behind disagreements between people groups, an examination of this letter seems to reveal a shift in attitude. On behalf of the Church, Constantine takes offense at the religious Jews who deny Jesus and His resurrection. However, it appears he moved beyond a reasonable theological disagreement into a disparaging personal opinion of Jews.

The Emperor's description of the Jews as a people who "had soiled their hands with the most fearful of crimes and whose minds were blinded" has biblical grounds. As we have seen in the New Testament, unbelieving Jews were accused of complicity in the crucifixion of

---

[9] *On the Keeping of Easter*, Found in Eusebius, *Vita Const.*, Lib. iii., 18–20.

Jesus (Acts 2:23, 3:13-18) and were veiled and hardened (Rom 11:25, 2 Cor 3:14-16). However, Constantine's stated desire "to separate ourselves from the detestable company of the Jews" is problematic.

Because every other comment in this letter has the observance of Easter as its subject, it is reasonable to interpret this remark as similarly focused. In other words, we could construe the Emperor's meaning as, "we do not want the celebration of Christ's resurrection connected to a holiday celebrated by those who deny Christ." The sentiment of separating Christian observances from deniers of Christ perhaps shows a noble sense of piety and esteem for Jesus. However, Constantine's desire to separate from the "detestable company of the Jews" reveals an unbiblical stance toward non-Christians. It is not very Christ-like. (Imagine if Jesus had chosen to separate Himself from the detestable company of sinners!) In this statement, Constantine goes beyond a mere theological need to distinguish Christianity from Judaism. He is promoting a distancing of Christians from the Jewish people.

Constantine's statement also suggests a lack of comprehension regarding the continuity between Judaism and Christ. This was something the early Christian writers had up until then affirmed. It is no coincidence Jesus celebrated His Last Supper as a Passover Seder. His death and resurrection occurred during the very Pesach holiday that had been foretelling His passion for over a millennium. Thus, while choosing a date other than 14 Nisan to celebrate the Resurrection was not unbiblical, it seems perhaps narrow-minded in hindsight.

As the de facto head of the Christian Church at the time, one would hope for a more biblical tone from the Emperor, one that communicates an earnest desire for the salvation of the Jews. More appropriate would have been a Christ-like posture that encouraged love and prayer for the Jews despite (perhaps *because of*) their chosen position as enemies of Christ. But Constantine, who was raised a pagan, had only become a Christian a few years earlier. He was an outsider stepping into a family dynasty (so to speak) that predated him by centuries. He found himself caught up in a sort of sibling rivalry between Jews and Christians. But not as an equal. Rather than one of the quarreling siblings, Constantine was in a position of authority. He was more like a step-father who married into the unrest. And he did not approach the conflict like a natural father would, encouraging unity between his rival sons. Instead, as the new step-father, blind to the history and nuances of the relationship, he chose sides.

That said, there was a legitimate need for the Church to establish its boundaries at that time in history. From a modern perspective, it is easy to view this ancient conflict as an oversimplified Jew versus Christian issue. But Jewish scholar Daniel Boyarin cautions us that the religious identities in antiquity were less sure than we think:

> The very terms of identity were being worked on and worked out. Not only had there not been a divided "parting of the ways," but Christianity was deeply engaged in finding its identity, it's boundaries, and even busily and noisily sorting out what kind of an entity it would be, what kind of an identity it would form.[10]

It was likely this socio-political need that drove the Church to assertively mark its borderlines. And, in some cases, to overreach in that effort.

Notably, the Nicene ruling did not offer any specific directive for determining the date of Easter.[11] Constantine only wrote, "all our

---

[10] Daniel Boyarin, *Borderlines: The Partition of Judaeo-Christianity* (Philadelphia, PA: University of Pennsylvania Press, 2004), p. xi.

[11] In the centuries following Nicaea, numerous attempts were made at calculating a date for Easter that all of Christendom could affirm. It was not until the early ninth century under Charles the Great that a calculation was unanimously adopted. Schaff & Wace (1997) note, "It is curious that after all the attempts that have been made to get this matter settled, the Church is still separated into East and West—the latter having accepted the Gregorian Calendar from which the Eastern Church, still using the Julian Calendar, differs in being twelve days behind. And even in the West we have succeeded in breaking the spirit of the Nicene decree, for in 1825 the Christian Easter coincided with the Jewish Passover!"

brethren in the East . . . are henceforth to celebrate the said most sacred feast of Easter at the same time with the Romans and yourselves." The goal was not to instruct Christendom when Easter was to be observed but rather ensure it was observed in unity.

The Council of Nicaea ultimately closed with the theology of the New Testament fundamentally uncorrupted. However, the Christian attitudes toward Jews and Judaism had begun drifting. And in the evolution of the Christian Church in the centuries following Nicaea, we, unfortunately, find outright anti-Semitism beginning to rear its ugly head. So, rather than the culmination of centuries of growing anti-Semitism within Christianity, the Council of Nicaea perhaps marked its beginning. One could make the argument that Christianity's evolution from a persecuted faith in the early centuries to a religion in power brought with it many unfortunate and unbiblical side effects. But that is a discussion for a different day.

CHAPTER 5

Conclusion

OUR GOAL WAS TO DETERMINE IF, by the conclusion of the Council of Nicaea, Christian theology had been altered or corrupted due to anti-Jewish attitudes. And if so, how, and to what extent, was it altered. While anti-Jewish attitudes did exist, we saw that they did not corrupt or negatively alter Christian theology to any appreciable degree. For a portion of Christendom, anti-Jewish sentiment played a direct role by impacting the date they observed the Resurrection. However, as we saw, because Easter is not a festival mandated by Scripture, the date of its observance is a church matter rather than a theological issue.[1]

Concerning the biblical position Christians should hold on Jews and Judaism, we established a five-point framework based on the New Testament teachings. Christians are to:

1. Recognize Israel's central role in God's story
2. Acknowledge the failure of the Jewish religious leadership
3. Reject Jewish teachings that deny Christ
4. Understand Israel's future salvation
5. Love and earnestly desire the salvation of Jews

The theology reflected in the early Christian writings we looked at aligns remarkably well with this framework. And the Council of

---

[1] This is perhaps analogous to discussing changing the date of Hanukkah today. There would be strong opinions and appeals to history. However, neither side could claim theological or Scriptural grounds for their position.

Nicaea did not deviate from that theology. Where we saw a change over time is in the Christian *attitudes* toward the Jewish people. In particular, Constantine issued some troublesome and irresponsible statements on behalf of the council regarding the motivation to "separate ourselves from the detestable company of the Jews." The decision to prohibit Christian communities from commemorating the Resurrection on 14 Nisan if they so chose was not made on biblical grounds. Nevertheless, whatever Constantine or the early Church may have felt about the Jewish people, it did not corrupt the theology handed down by Jesus and the Apostles.

There was also no notable effort by the Church to distance Christianity from its Jewish roots. In fact, there was unanimous agreement on two important facts: (1.) the Jewish Bible is inspired Scripture, and (2.) Christianity is a continuation of the Story that began therein. The Church Fathers of one accord saw Jesus as the Jewish Mashiach foretold in the Hebrew Bible. Moreover, early Christian writers esteemed the Tanakh and studied it judiciously.

For example, in a letter written around AD 230, the influential Church father Origen goes into great detail explaining where the Septuagint (Greek) version of the Old Testament differed from the Hebrew version. He declared:

> When we notice such things, we are forthwith to reject as spurious the copies in use in our Churches, and enjoin the brotherhood to put away the sacred books current among them, and to coax the Jews, and persuade them to give us copies which shall be untampered with and free from forgery![2]

---

[2] Origen (ca. AD 230), *A Letter from Origen to Africanus*, 4.

Further, in his apologetic against Celsus, Origen defends the Jews as a learned nation on par with the Egyptians, Syrians, and other nations.[3]

CLOSING THOUGHTS

Allow me to share a few closing thoughts. These are observations relevant to our discussion that did not fit neatly into the flow of our study but are worth considering.

On Terminology

To fully deal with the question before us, we need to consider an additional factor not previously mentioned—namely, the proper meaning of the term *anti-Jewish*. Throughout this book, a number of similar, related words have been used that can confuse rather than clarify the discussion: *Israel, Jews, Hebrews, Jewish, Judaism, anti-Semitism*. The danger in this imprecise terminology is revealed by a single question: *Who is a Jew?* Without context, it is difficult to even define the category of this question. Is it ethnic? Religious? National? Cultural? The Oxford English Dictionary defines a *Jew* as,

> A member of the people and cultural community whose traditional religion is Judaism and who trace their origins through the ancient Hebrew people of Israel to Abraham.

Who, then, is a *Hebrew*?

> A member of an ancient people living in what is now Israel and Palestine and, according to biblical tradition, descended from the patriarch Jacob, grandson of Abraham. After the Exodus they established the kingdoms of Israel and Judah, and their scriptures and traditions form

---

[3] Origen, *Contra Celsus*, Book I, Ch. XIV.

the basis of the Jewish religion. (Oxford English Dictionary)

Who, then, is *Israel*? The term "Israel" refers to the ancient kingdom or its religious leadership. It can also refer to the modern nation-state. Or the Jewish people as a whole.

It is evident that, on this issue, categories run together, blend, and overlap. We cannot cleanly dissect the ethnic, religious, national, cultural, and historical aspects of Jewishness. Nor should we. They are all part of one people and one history. The Hebrew language is a language of ancient faith that even today cannot be taught apart from sacred Scripture. Indeed, *Jewishness* is a beautiful, ornate, complex tapestry comprised of a shared history, a culture, a people, a language, and a religion. Thus, there is an irreducible level of inherent ambiguity in the discussion.

Epilogue on the Christian's Biblical View of Jews

How are followers of Jesus to properly view Jews and Judaism? As Christians, Scripture must determine our position. And, as we have established, the Bible teaches that Judaism cannot be utterly dismissed or wholly embraced by Christians. A biblical response is a nuanced response that necessarily contains a tension.

The parts of Jewishness that Christians must accept include Jewish history, the Jewish people, and the Jewish Scriptures. These are all affirmed in the New Testament. Indeed, it is the very Jewish history, people, and Story into which Christians have been adopted. What, then, must Christians reject? First, we must reject anti-Semitism as morally repugnant and unbiblical. We are also required to reject those tenets of Judaism that reject Jesus. And what of the Law of Moses? Christians certainly must accept it as an integral part of Scripture and the history of God's people. Indeed, Paul had the entire Jewish Bible in view when he wrote:

> All Scripture is breathed out by God and profitable for teaching, for reproof, for correction, and for training in righteousness, that the man of God may be complete, equipped for every good work. (2 Timothy 3:16-17)

However, like Israel's slavery in Egypt, her covenant given at Sinai, and her exile in Babylon, the Law of Moses was not intended to last forever. It was given as a tutor or a guardian to guide the nation of Israel until Christ came.[4]

The Jewish teaching that Jesus was neither divine nor the Messiah is simply wrong. Jesus rejected it. The New Testament authors opposed it. And we need to resist it, too. To wholly accept Judaism is to wholly deny Christ. Yet, conversely, to wholly accept Christ does not require a complete rejection of Judaism. As the apostle Paul modeled, a Jew does not need to leave their Jewishness behind to follow Jesus. In fact, Messianic Jews (Jewish believers in Jesus) often refer to themselves as *completed Jews*.

As Christians, our fight is not with the Jewish people or with "Jewishness" in general. It's not even with the religion of Judaism as a whole. Our conflict is solely with the teachings of Jewish theology that deny our Savior. And that can be a tricky balance to maintain. Faith is a vital and intensely personal affair. Offense can lie just below the surface and is easily triggered. The apostle Peter gives us some guidance:

> Have no fear of them, nor be troubled, but in your hearts honor Christ the Lord as holy, always being prepared to make a defense to anyone who asks you for a reason for the hope that is in you; yet do it with gentleness and respect, having a good conscience, so that, when you are

---

[4] Luke 16:16; Galatians 3:24-25. See my book *Torahism* for an in-depth examination of this subject.

slandered, those who revile your good behavior in Christ may be put to shame. For it is better to suffer for doing good, if that should be God's will, than for doing evil. (1 Peter 3:14-17)

On Freedom

Whatever God creates or decrees is perfect. And then we humans get our hands on it. God created mankind innocent, and we fell into sin. God gave the Law at Sinai, and His people broke it even before Moses came down from the mountain. Likewise, God gave us His Word knowing we would not discern its meaning in perfect agreement. Thankfully, there is freedom in Christ. Paul wrote:

> Therefore let no one pass judgment on you in questions of food and drink, or with regard to a festival or a new moon or a Sabbath. (Colossians 2:16)

In other words, regarding these things, followers of Jesus are free to choose as a matter of conscience. "Now the Lord is the Spirit, and where the Spirit of the Lord is, there is freedom" (2 Cor 3:17). However, "All things are lawful, but not all things are helpful. All things are lawful, but not all things build up" (1 Cor 10:23). Therefore, "do not use your freedom as an opportunity for the flesh, but through love serve one another" (Gal 5:13b). Indeed, "Live as people who are free, not using your freedom as a cover-up for evil, but living as servants of God" (1 Pet 2:16).

Seeking a Biblical Tone

Scripture has much to say about how we deal with our opponents. We are to value mercy, forgiveness, turning the other cheek, and praying for those who persecute us. The Bible also models harsh criticisms against "the wicked." This confrontational component is evident in Jesus' cleansings of the temple and woes against the Pharisees. There we find no semblance of gentleness or diplomacy. This tone is also apparent at times in the Psalms. The psalmist often asks God to mete out severe punishment on his enemies:

> *O God, break the teeth in their mouths;*
>   *tear out the fangs of the young lions, O Lord! . . .*
> *Let them be like the snail that dissolves into slime,*
>   *like the stillborn child who never sees the sun.*
> *Sooner than your pots can feel the heat of thorns,*
>   *whether green or ablaze, may he sweep them away!*
> *The righteous will rejoice when he sees the vengeance;*
>   *he will bathe his feet in the blood of the wicked.*
> (Psalm 58:6-10)

The severe sentiment in this and other passages is markedly different from loving our enemies and praying for those who persecute us. What can be concluded from this?

Some argue Scripture was a "product of its time," written in a turbulent era when survival and conquest were paramount. Modern culture, by contrast, values tolerance, inclusion, and non-judgmentalism. However, any contemporary reading of the Bible is also a "product of its time." The question we need to ask is: what does God want us to take away from the range of biblical teachings about dealing with opponents?

Scripture consistently presents an unmistakable moral distinction between good and evil, the righteous and the wicked, right and wrong. This contrast extends to faith in Christ, who taught, "Whoever is not with me is against me, and whoever does not gather with me scatters" (Matt 12:30).[5] Indeed, when Jesus sent out the twelve, He told them:

---

[5] See also Mark 9:40; Luke 9:50, 11:23.

If the house is worthy, let your peace come upon it, but if it is not worthy, let your peace return to you. And if anyone will not receive you or listen to your words, shake off the dust from your feet when you leave that house or town. (Matthew 10:13-14)

The Lord required His followers to exercise judgment in determining the worthiness of the house. And He was not referring to the moral standing of the occupants but their willingness to receive His disciples and listen to their words. And if the house was unwilling? Jesus commanded His followers to take back their peace and perform the symbolic act of shaking the dust off their feet, which "was a renunciation and indicated a severed relationship."[6] Moreover, Jesus cautioned that those who deny Him or are ashamed of Him, He will, in turn, be ashamed of and deny before the Father.[7]

Perhaps the thread connecting these biblical denunciations of "the wicked" is that they target those who are willfully and knowingly rebelling against God. Jesus did not criticize the woman at the well or the rich young ruler the way He did the Pharisees, who knew better and resisted His message. Therefore, there seems to be biblical precedent regarding the strong opposition expressed by the early Christians we read about in this book. Men like Justin and Cyprian were opposing the Jews who were willfully and knowingly denying Christ.

There is a seriousness in Christ's self-understanding that modern believers can tend to overlook in favor of His love and mercy. In gazing on His astounding loveliness, we can miss his equally important holiness. In trying to love and hope the best for others, we sometimes fail to recognize those in open rebellion against God and His message.

---

[6] John D Barry et al., *Faithlife Study Bible: Intriguing Insights to Inform Your Faith* (Grand Rapids, Michigan: Zondervan, 2012), *Matthew 10:14*. (See also Mark 6:11; Luke 9:5; Acts 13:51.).

[7] Mark 8:38. See also Luke 12:8-9; 1 John 2:23; 2 Timothy 2:12.

Consider Jesus' warning placed in the middle of His teaching on how to rightly judge: "Do not give dogs what is holy, and do not throw your pearls before pigs, lest they trample them underfoot and turn to attack you" (Matt 7:6).

Taken holistically, Scripture teaches that, in addition to love, mercy, and forgiveness, there is also a time for opposition and a time for separation. How do we know which is which? Theologian Reinhold Niebuhr offers a prayerful approach in what is popularly known as the Serenity Prayer: "God, grant me the serenity to accept the things I cannot change, courage to change the things I can, and wisdom to know the difference."

IN SUMMARY

There is a growing interest in the Jewish roots of the Christian faith and a desire to understand Scripture in its Middle Eastern cultural context. Perhaps the emergence in recent decades of the "name it and claim it" movement, the prosperity gospel, and progressive Christianity (with its peddling of Bonhoeffer's "cheap grace"[8]) has left Christians thirsting for substance. There is much to be admired about the quest for the historical and theological roots of our faith. In fact, movements like *Torahism* may be a healthy warning sign. They may represent a countering of the Western Church's drift toward a commercialized, watered-down faith.

However, caution must be urged. In the second century, Marcion swung the pendulum too far. By rejecting the Jews and their Scriptures, he ended up drowning in heresy and was ejected from the Church. Today *Torahism* is swinging the pendulum too far in the other

---

[8] Eric Metaxas, *Pastor, Martyr, Prophet, Spy: Pastor, Martyr, Prophet, Spy.* (Thomas Nelson, 2010), p. 263.

direction. By declaring the laws given to Israel under the Sinai covenant are binding on Christians—who were never included in the Sinai covenant in the first place—Torahism, too, is wading into heresy. We need to pursue a healthy, biblical balance. Recognizing and honoring the true Jewish roots of the Christian faith is an effort worth making. The Gospel, after all, is a Jewish story.

From the Author

Thank you for taking the time to read this book! I appreciate your interest in this important topic, and I pray you found something here that enlightened or encouraged you. If you have questions, thoughts, or feedback, I'd love to hear from you. You can reach me on social media or email me directly at rls@rlsolberg.com. I try my best to respond to all correspondence.

Also, if you enjoyed the book, would you consider submitting a review on Amazon.com? Just look for the Customer Reviews section on the product page for *Divergence*. It would mean a lot to me personally, as well as help to spread the word. Thank you!

Grace & Peace,

R. L. Solberg
RLSolberg.com
DivergenceBook.com

Name & Subject Index

I

Ignatius, 4, 65, 129, 130, 145
intertestamental period, 41
Isaac, 16, 52
Isaiah (prophet), 17, 18, 27, 31,
    41, 89, 146, 159
Ishmael, 16

J

Jacob, 16, 18, 73, 87, 111, 159,
    162
Jamieson, Robert, 24, 44, 130
Jehne, Martin, 6
Jerusalem, 4, 8, 11, 13, 14, 18, 23,
    26, 30, 38, 46, 52, 53, 56, 58,
    74, 84, 93, 146, 150, 155, 160,
    164
Jerusalem Council, 42, 88
Jewish Christians, 5, 43, 60, 61,
    72, 90, 93
Jewish religious leaders, 25, 26,
    28, 43, 56, 60, 102
Jewish religious leadership, 29,
    33, 38, 90, 102, 109
Jewishness, 14, 31, 80, 112, 113
Jonah, 51
Joseph, 51, 158, 159, 163
Judea, 57, 59, 60

L

Landman, Isaac, 11, 12, 37, 131
Last Supper, 49, 51, 94, 105
leitourgia, 47
Lincoln, Andrew, 92, 131
Lord's Day, 2, 40, 46-48, 49, 66,
    91, 92, 103, 129
Lord's Prayer, 89

Lord's Supper, 47, 51, 52, 53, 94,
    95
Luther, Martin, 6, 15

M

Maccabaeus, Judas, 53
Manasseh, 8
manmade traditions, 52, 53, 95
Marcion, 66, 67, 68, 69, 70, 101,
    117, 145
Marcionism, 5, 65, 66, 68, 70,
    129
markers, theological, 2, 40, 66,
    91, 102
Martyr, Justin, 65, 71-78, 83, 90,
    94, 116, 146
Martyrdom, 4, 146
Mashiach, 35, 37, 57, 58, 90
Melito, 65, 78-83, 90, 130, 146,
    149
Moreschini, Claudio, 83, 131

N

Nazarenes, 13, 58, 61
Nazareth, 19, 27, 59
Neapolis, 71
Nero, 3, 63
New Covenant, 36, 42, 51, 53, 55,
    71, 95
new moon, 42, 114
Nicaea, 5, 2, 40, 55, 97-103, 106,
    107, 109-110, 131
Nicene Creed, 100, 101
Niebuhr, Reinhold, 117
Nisan, 78, 93, 94, 105, 110
Noah, 51, 162
Numbers, 31

O

Oden, Thomas, 101, 131
On the Keeping of Easter, 103
On the Pascha, 5, 6, 65, 78-82,
  149
Origen, 110, 111, 147

P

Palestine, 56, 60, 111
Pamphilus of Caesarea, 102
Paschal lamb. *See* Passover lamb
Passover, 1, 2, 40, 49-53, 66, 78-
  82, 93-95, 99, 103, 105-106,
  131, 149, 150-151, 155, 158-
  159, 165
Passover lamb, 50, 51, 93
patriarchs, Jewish, 16, 17, 22, 24,
  78, 158
Pentecost, 38, 49, 74, 103
Pesach. *See* Passover
Peter (Apostle), 18, 19, 32, 38,
  42, 50, 52, 74, 75, 88, 113,
  143, 145, 146, 147
Peter of Alexandria, 102
Pharisee(s), 14, 26, 29, 30, 35, 43,
  44, 58, 115, 116, 131, 133,
  134, 135, 136
Polycarp, 68, 145-146
Pompey, 56, 57
Pope Victor I, 94
Price, Rose, 6
progressive Christianity, 117
pro-Jewish, 81
Prophets, the, 31, 37, 80
prosperity gospel, 117

Q

Quartodeciman(s), 78, 80, 94

R

rabbinic Judaism, 38
race, iii, 8, 16, 20, 49, 63, 92, 104
  racial, 6, 7, 8
  racial relations, 3, 6
  racial theory, iii, 7, 9, 12
  racism, 7, 12, 99
Rebekah, 86, 87
Reformation, 6
religio illicita, 3
religio licita, 3
remnant, Jewish, 17, 20, 76
Roman Empire, 3, 4, 5, 63, 97,
  129
Rome, 3, 4, 6, 23, 36, 57, 59, 62,
  63, 68, 129, 146, 147, 168
Rosen, Dr. Moishe, 49, 50, 93,
  131

S

Sabbath, ii, 1, 2, 27, 40-49, 61,
  66, 72, 91-93, 99, 103, 114,
  129, 131, 133, 134, 140
sacrifice, 49, 50, 52, 79, 82, 85,
  149, 150, 153, 155, 159, 161
Sadducees, 26, 31, 58, 134
Samaritan(s), 8, 71
Samuel the Small, 60
Sandmel, Rabbi Samuel, 35, 131
Sanhedrin, 15, 56, 75, 136
Sarah, 38
Schaff, Philip, 56, 57, 84, 85, 89,
  98, 106, 131

Bibliography

Alexander, P. S. (1999). The Parting of the Ways from the Perspective of Rabbinic Judaism. In J. D. G. Dunn (Ed.), *Jews and Christians: The Parting of the Ways AD 70 to 135*. Eerdmans Publishing Company. (Original work published 1989)

Andrei, M. (2018, August 24). *In Ancient Rome, Political Discourse Was Sometimes Like an Internet Fight*. ZME Science. https://www.zmescience.com/science/history-science/rome-political-discourse-insults-24082018/

Babcock, B. C., Barry, J. D., Brown, D. R., & Klippenstein, R. (Eds.). (2016). *The Lexham Bible Dictionary*. Lexham Press.

Baer, Y. (1961). "Israel, The Christian Church, And the Roman Empire from the Time of The Spetimius Severus To the Edict of Toleration of AD 313." In A. Fuks, I. Halpern (Eds.), *Studies in History*. Magnes Press.

Barnett, P. (1999). *Jesus and the Rise of Early Christianity: A History of New Testament Times*. Intervarsity Press.

Barry, J. D., Mangum, D., Brown, D. R., Heiser, M. S., Custis, M., & Ritzema, E. (2012). *Faithlife Study Bible: Intriguing Insights to Inform Your Faith*. Zondervan.

Bennett, R. (2002). *Four Witnesses: The Early Church in Her Own Words*. Ignatius Press.

Berdyaev, N. (1928). *Marcionism*. www.berdyaev.com. http://www.berdyaev.com/berdiaev/berd_lib/1928_336.html

Boyarin, D. (2004). *Borderlines: The Partition of Judaeo-Christianity*. University of Pennsylvania Press.

Carson, D. A. (1999). *From Sabbath to Lord's Day: A Biblical, Historical, and Theological Investigation*. Wipf And Stock Publishers.

Chadwick, H. (1993). *The Early Church*. Penguin Books.

Chapman, H. P. (1908). "St. Cyprian of Carthage." In C. Herbermann (Ed.), *Catholic Encyclopedia* (vol. 4, pp. 694–695). Robert Appleton Company.

Cohen, S. J. D. (1980). "A Virgin Defiled: Some Rabbinic and Christian Views on The Origins Of Heresy." In Union Seminary Quarterly Review, 36 (1), pp. 1-11.

Cohen, S. J. D. (2014). *From the Maccabees to the Mishnah*. Westminster John Knox Press.

Elwell, W. A., & Beitzel, B. J. (1988). *Baker Encyclopedia of the Bible* (Vol. 2). Baker.

Eshel, H. (2006). "The Bar Kochba Revolt, 132-135." *The Cambridge History of Judaism, Volume 4, the Late Roman-Rabbinic Period*, pp. 105–127.

Ferguson, E. (2013). *Church History: The Rise and Growth of the Church in Its Cultural, Intellectual, and Political Context* (Vol. 1). Zondervan.

Fox, R. L. (2006). *Pagans and Christians in the Mediterranean World: From the Second Century AD to the Conversion of Constantine*. Penguin.

Fried, L. S. (2014). *Ezra and the Law in History and Tradition*. University Of South Carolina.

Hanneken, T. R. (1997). A Completely Different Reading of Melito's Peri Pascha. *Meqorot: The University of Chicago Journal of Jewish Studies*, (3), pp. 26-33.

Hodge, C. H. (1835). "A Commentary on Romans" in *The Geneva Series of Commentaries*. Banner of Truth Trust (1974).

Horbury, W. (1982). The Benediction of the Minim and Early Jewish-Christian Controversy. *The Journal of Theological Studies*, XXXIII (1), 19–61. https://doi.org/10.1093/jts/xxxiii.1.19

Ignatius. (1968). *Epistle to the Romans* (M. Staniforth, Trans.). Dorset Press. (Original work published ca. ad 110)

Jamieson, R., Fausset, A. R., & Brown, D. (1997). *A Commentary Critical and Explanatory on the Whole Bible* (Vol. 2). Logos Research Systems, Inc.

Kimelman, R. (1981). "Birkat Ha-minim and the Lack of Evidence for an Anti-Christian Jewish Prayer in Late Antiquity." In Sanders, E. P.; Baumgarten, A. I. (eds.), *Jewish and Christian Self-Definition*, Volume 2, pp. 226-244.

Landman, I., & Cohen, S. (1969). *The Universal Jewish Encyclopedia: The Seven-Branched Light; A Reading Guide and Index to the Universal Jewish Encyclopedia.* New York, Ktav Pub. House.

Lincoln, A. T. (1999). "From Sabbath to Lord's Day: A Biblical and Theological Perspective." In D. A. Carson (Ed.), *From Sabbath to Lord's Day: A Biblical, Historical and Theological Investigation.* Wipf and Stock Publishers.

Martyr, J. (1885). *Dialogue with Trypho* (A. Roberts, J. Donaldson, Eds., G. Reith, Trans.). T & T Clark. (Original work published ca. ad 160)

Metaxas, E. (2010). *Bonhoeffer: Pastor, Martyr, Prophet, Spy.* Thomas Nelson.

Moreschini, C., & Norelli, E. (2005). *Early Christian Greek and Latin Literature: A Literary History from the Council of Nicea to the Beginning of the Medieval Period* (Vol. 2). Hendrickson Publishers.

Lexico. (2019). Jew. In *Lexico.com dictionary.* Retrieved April 27, 2021, from https://www.lexico.com/en/definition/jew

Lexico. (2019). Hebrew. In *Lexico.com dictionary.* Retrieved April 27, 2021, from https://www.lexico.com/en/definition/hebrew

Oden, T. C. (2011). "The Faith Once Delivered: Nicaea and Evangelic Confession." In T. George (Ed.), *Evangelicals and Nicene Faith: Reclaiming the Apostolic Witness.* Baker Publishing Group.

Rosen, C., & Rosen, M. (2006). *Christ in the Passover.* Moody Publishers.

Sandmel, S. (2005). *A Jewish Understanding of the New Testament.* Jewish Lights Pub.

Schaff, P. (2004). *Fathers of the Third Century: Hippolytus, Cyprian, Caius, Novatian, Appendix.* Christian Classics Ethereal Library. (Original work published 1885)

Schaff, P., & Wace, H. (Eds.). (1997). *A Select Library of Nicene and Post-Nicene fathers of the Christian Church* (Vol. 14). T & T Clark. (Original work published 1890)

Segal, A. F. (1992). *Paul the Convert: The Apostolate and Apostasy of Saul the Pharisee.* Yale University Press.

Smallwood, E. M. (1976). *The Jews Under Roman Rule from Pompeii to Diocletian*. Leiden.

Smith, C., & Covino, R. (2011). *Praise and Blame in Roman Republican Rhetoric*. Classical Press of Wales.

Solberg, R. L. (2019). *Torahism: Are Christians Required to Keep the Law of Moses?* Williamson College Press.

Staniforth, M. (1968). *Early Christian Writings: The Apostolic Fathers*. Dorset Press.

Stott, J. R. W. (1994). *The Message of Romans*. Intervarsity Press.

Strong, A. H. (2009). *Systematic Theology: A Compendium Designed for the Use of Theological Students*. Judson Press. (Original work published 1903)

Studer, B., & Louth, A. (1993). *Trinity and Incarnation: The Faith of the Early Church*. Liturgical Press.

Suetonius. (2006). *Lives of the Twelve Caesars* (A. Thomson, Trans.). Project Gutenberg. (Original work published ca. ad 121)

Tertullian. (1972). *Adversus Marcionem* (E. Evans, Trans.). Oxford University Press. (Original work published ca. ad 208)

Wax, T. (2013, January 28). "Why Did Jesus Say He Came Only for Israel?" The Gospel Coalition. www.thegospelcoalition.org/blogs/trevin-wax/why-did-jesus-say-he-came-only-for- israel

Wiersbe, W. W. (1996). *The Bible Exposition Commentary* (Vol. 2). Victor Books.

Wiersbe, W. W. (2011). *The Wiersbe Bible Study Series. Romans 1:18–3:20*. David C. Cook.

Wessel, W. W. (1984). *The Expositor's Bible Commentary* (F. E. Gaebelein, Ed.; Vol. 8). Zondervan Publishing House.

Wright, N. T. (2004). *The Climax of the Covenant: Christ and the Law in Pauline Theology*. T & T Clark.

Appendix A

INSTANCES OF THE PERSECUTION OF JESUS AS RECORDED IN THE GOSPELS

Passage	Persecutors (ESV)	Nature	Notes
Luke 4:28-30	Everyone in the synagogue	Moved against Him	Tried to throw Him off a cliff
Matt 9:3; Mark 2:6-7; Luke 5:21-24	Pharisees, Scribes	Questioned/challenged Him	Re: Healing a paralytic
Matt 9:11-14; Mark 2:16-18; Luke 5:30-33	Pharisees, Scribes	Questioned/challenged Him	Re: Fasting
Matt 9:34	Pharisees	Questioned/challenged Him	Re: Power of demons
Matt 12:1-8; Mark 2:23-28; Luke 6:1-5	Pharisees	Questioned/challenged Him	Re: Sabbath
Matt 12:9-14; Mark 3:1-6; Luke 6:6-11	Pharisees, Scribes	Plotted against Him	Re: To kill Him
Matt 12:24-28; Mark 3:22-26	Pharisees, Scribes	Questioned/challenged Him	Re: Power of demons
Matt 15:1-3a; Mark 7:1-23	Pharisees, Scribes	Questioned/challenged Him	Re: Traditions of cleanliness
Matt 16:1-4; Mark 8:9-12	Pharisees, Sadducees	Questioned/challenged Him	Demanded signs

Passage	Persecutors (ESV)	Nature	Notes
Matt 19:1-12; Mark 10:1-12	Pharisees	Questioned/challenged Him	Re: Divorce
John 5:18	The Jews	Plotted against Him	For breaking Sabbath and making Himself equal with God
John 7:1	The Jews	Plotted against Him	To kill Him
John 7:30-36, 45-52	Pharisees, Chief Priests	Moved against Him	Tried to arrest Him
John 8:48-59	Pharisees, Chief Priests	Moved against Him	Challenged His identity, tried to stone Him
John 9:22	The Jews	Moved against Him	Believers put out of the Synagogue
Luke 7:36-39	Pharisees	Questioned/challenged Him	Re: Forgiving the sinful woman
Luke 11:53-54	Pharisees, Scribes	Plotted against Him	To catch Him in something He might say
Luke 13:14-17	The ruler of the synagogue	Questioned/challenged Him	Re: Sabbath
John 10:31-39	The Jews	Moved against Him	Attempted to stone and arrest Him
John 11:45-57	Pharisees, Chief Priests	Plotted against Him	To kill Him
Luke 16:14	Pharisees	Moved against Him	Ridiculed/mocked Him

Passage	Persecutors (ESV)	Nature	Notes
John 12:9-11	Chief Priests	Moved against Him	Made plans to kill resurrected Lazarus (he was causing many to believe in Jesus)
Mark 11:18; Luke 19:47-48	Chief Priests, Scribes, Principal men of the people	Plotted against Him	To kill Him
Matt 21:23-27; Mark 11:27-33; Luke 20:1-8	Chief Priests, Scribes, Elders of the people	Questioned/challenged Him	Re: His authority
Matt 21:45-46; Mark 12:12-17	Pharisees, Chief Priests, some of the Herodians	Plotted against Him	To arrest Him
Matt 22:15-22; Mark 12:13-17; Luke 20:19-26	Pharisees, Scribes, Chief Priests, some of the Herodians	Questioned/challenged Him	Re: Paying taxes to Caesar
Matt 22:34-40; Mark 12:28-34	Pharisees, Scribes	Questioned/challenged Him	Re: Greatest commandment
Matt 26:3-5; Mark 14:1-2; Luke 22:2	Chief Priests, Elders, Scribes	Plotted against Him	To kill Him
Matt 26:14-16; Mark 14:10-11; Luke 22:4-6	Chief priests, Officers	Plotted against Him	Judas' betrayal
Matt 26:47-56; Mark 14:43-52; Luke	Chief Priests, Officers, Elders,	Moved against Him	Jesus' betrayal and arrest

Passage	Persecutors (ESV)	Nature	Notes
22:47-53; John 18:2-12	Pharisees, Scribes		
Matt 26:57, 59-68; Mark 14:53, 55-65; Luke 22:54, 63-65; John 18:19-24	High Priest, Scribes, Elders, Chief Priests, Whole Council, Men holding Jesus	Moved against Him	Mocked, beaten before Sanhedrin
Luke 22:66-71	Elders of the people, Chief Priests, Scribes	Moved against Him	Bound and delivered Him to Pilate
Matt 27:1-2, 11-14; Mark 15:1-5; Luke 23:1-5; John 18:28-32	Chief Priests, Elders, Scribes, Whole Council, the Jews, the crowds	Moved against Him	Brought Him before Pilate and falsely accused Him, demanded His death
Luke 23:10-11	Chief Priests, Scribes	Moved against Him	Falsely accusing Him
Matt 27:20-26; Mark 15:11-15; Luke 23:18-25; John 18:40, 19:5-12	Chief Priests, Elders, the crowd/people, the rulers, the Jews, Officers	Moved against Him	Brought Him before Pilate and falsely accused Him, demanded His death
Matt 27:41-43; Mark 15:31-32; Luke 23:35	Chief Priests, Scribes, Elders, the rulers	Moved against Him	Ridiculed/mocked Him on the cross
Matt 28:11-15	Chief priests	Moved against Him	Paid Romans to lie about Jesus' body

Appendix B

THE TEN COMMANDMENTS AS REFERENCED IN THE NEW TESTAMENT

Torah Commandment	Related NT Teachings / Passages
You shall have no other gods before Me	"...Worship the Lord your God, and serve him only" (Matthew 4:10)
	"...Worship the Lord your God and serve him only." (Luke 4:8)
	"They exchanged the truth about God for a lie, and worshiped and served created things rather than the Creator..." (Romans 1:25)
	Also see Acts 7:39-43, 17:16-34; 2 Thessalonians 2:4; Revelation 9:20, 13:4.
You shall not make idols	"Dear children, keep yourselves from idols." (1 John 5:21)
	"Do not be idolaters..." (1 Corinthians 10:7)
	"...you must not associate with anyone who claims to be a brother or sister but is . . . an idolater ..." (1 Corinthians 5:11)
	Also see Acts 17:16; 1 Corinthians 6:9, 8:4; Revelations 9:20.
You shall not take the name of the LORD your God in vain	" ...Our Father in heaven, hallowed be your name..." (Matthew 6:9)
	"...many will come in my name, claiming, 'I am he,' and, 'The time is near.' Do not follow them'" (Luke 21:8)

	"Don't let anyone look down on you because you are young, but set an example for the believers in speech…" (1 Timothy 4:12)
	Also see Mark 3:29; Luke 12:10; Acts 4:12; Ephesians 5:4; Titus 2:7-8; 2 Thessalonians 1:12; 2 Timothy 2:19; Revelations 13:5-6.
Remember the Sabbath day, to keep it holy	The New Testament does not teach or repeat the commandments about keeping, remembering, or observing the Sabbath or about keeping it holy. There is this:
	"Then he said to them, 'The Sabbath was made for man, not man for the Sabbath. So the Son of Man is Lord even of the Sabbath.'" (Mark 2:27-28)
Honor your father and your mother *	"…honor your father and mother…" (Matthew 15:4)
	"…honor your father and mother…" (Mark 7:10)
	"…honor your father and mother." (Luke 18:20)
	Also see Matthew 19:19; Mark 10:19; Ephesians 6:2.
You shall not murder *	"…you shall not murder…" (Matthew 19:18)
	"…you shall not murder…" (Luke 18:20)
	"…you shall not murder…" (Romans 13:9)
	Also see Matthew 15:19.
You shall not commit adultery *	"You have heard that it was said, 'You shall not commit adultery.' But I tell you that anyone who looks at a woman lustfully has already committed adultery with her in his heart." (Matthew 5:27-28)

	"For out of the heart comes . . . adultery…" (Matthew 15:19)
	"…you shall not commit adultery…" (Matthew 19:18)
	Also see Matthew 5:32, 19:9; Mark 7:22, 10:12; Luke 18:20, Romans 13:9; 1 Corinthians 5:11, 6:9; Hebrews 13:4; James 2:11.
You shall not steal *	"…you shall not steal…" (Matthew 19:18)
	"…You shall not steal…" (Romans 13:9)
	"…you must not associate with anyone who claims to be a brother or sister but is . . . a swindler." (1 Corinthians 5:11)
	Also see Matthew 15:19; Luke 18:20.
You shall not bear false witness against your neighbor *	"For out of the heart comes . . . false testimony…" (Matthew 15:19)
	"…you shall not give false testimony…" (Matthew 19:18)
	"…must not associate with anyone who claims to be a brother or sister but is . . . a slanderer"(1 Corinthians 5:11)
	Also see Mark 7:22; Luke 18:20.
You shall not covet *	"…Be on your guard against all kinds of greed; life does not consist in an abundance of possessions" (Luke 12:15)
	"But sin, seizing the opportunity afforded by the commandment, produced in me every kind of coveting…" (Romans 7:8)
	"…You shall not covet…" (Romans 13:9)
	Also see Mark 7:22; Romans 1:29, 7:7; 1 Corinthians 6:10; Ephesians 5:5.

Repeated from the OT verbatim

Appendix C

LIST OF EARLY CHRISTIAN WRITINGS
DATED TO THE ANTE-NICENE ERA

This list of documents comes courtesy of the yeoman's work done by Peter Kirby to assemble a collection. Of the list, Kirby (n.d.) says,

> I have ordered [the documents] based on one possible chronological scheme. My judgments concerning the authenticity and dating of the documents concerned are made in the best tradition of biblical scholarship. Nevertheless, the ordering is almost certainly wrong in some part. To provide some bearings, a range of probable dating is provided for the scheme, but this range of dating can be disputed. All dates are approximate.

Each entry in the following list includes the estimated date of publication followed by document title. New Testament documents are shown in **bold**.

30-60	Passion Narrative	50-140	Oxyrhynchus 1224
40-80	Lost Sayings Gospel Q		Gospel
50-60	**1 Thessalonians**	50-150	Apocalypse of Adam
50-60	**Philippians**	50-150	Eugnostos the Blessed
50-60	**Galatians**	50-200	Sophia of Jesus Christ
50-60	**1 Corinthians**	**65-80**	**Gospel of Mark**
50-60	**2 Corinthians**	**70-100**	**Epistle of James**
50-60	**Romans**	70-120	Egerton Gospel
50-60	**Philemon**	70-160	Gospel of Peter
50-80	**Colossians**	70-160	Secret Mark
50-90	Signs Gospel	70-200	Fayyum Fragment
50-95	**Book of Hebrews**	70-200	Testaments of the
50-120	Didache		Twelve Patriarchs
50-140	Gospel of Thomas	73-200	Mara Bar Serapion
		80-100	**2 Thessalonians**

80-100	**Ephesians**	120-180	Apocryphon of John
80-100	**Gospel of Matthew**	120-180	Gospel of Mary
80-110	**1 Peter**	120-180	Dialogue of the Savior
80-120	Epistle of Barnabas	120-180	Gospel of the Savior
80-130	**Gospel of Luke**	120-180	2nd Apocalypse of
80-130	**Acts of the Apostles**		James
80-140	1 Clement	120-180	Trimorphic Protennoia
80-150	Gospel of the Egyptians	120-180	Gospel of Perfection
80-150	Gospel of the Hebrews	120-200	Genna Marias
80-250	Christian Sibyllines	130-140	Marcion
90-95	**Revelation**	130-150	Aristo of Pella
90-120	**Gospel of John**	130-160	Epiphanes On
90-120	**1 John**		Righteousness
90-120	**2 John**	130-160	Ophite Diagrams
90-120	**3 John**	130-160	2 Clement
90-120	**Epistle of Jude**	130-170	Gospel of Judas
93	Flavius Josephus	130-200	Epistle of Mathetes to
100-150	**1 Timothy**		Diognetus
100-150	**2 Timothy**	140-150	Epistula Apostolorum
100-150	**Titus**		
100-150	Apocalypse of Peter	140-160	Ptolemy
100-150	Secret Book of James	140-160	Isidore
100-150	Preaching of Peter	140-170	Fronto
100-160	Gospel of the Ebionites	140-170	Infancy Gospel of James
100-160	Gospel of the Nazoreans	140-170	Infancy Gospel of
100-160	Shepherd of Hermas		Thomas
100-160	**2 Peter**	140-180	Gospel of Truth
100-200	Odes of Solomon	150-160	Martyrdom of Polycarp
100-200	Gospel of Eve	150-160	Justin Martyr
100-230	Thunder, Perfect Mind	150-180	Excerpts of Theodotus
101-220	Book of Elchasai	150-180	Heracleon
105-115	Ignatius of Antioch	150-200	Ascension of Isaiah
110-140	Polycarp to the	150-200	Interpretation of
	Philippians		Knowledge
110-140	Papias	150-200	Testimony of Truth
110-160	Oxyrhynchus 840	150-200	Acts of Peter
	Gospel	150-200	Acts of John
110-160	Traditions of Matthias	150-200	Acts of Paul
111-112	Pliny the Younger	150-200	Acts of Andrew
115	Suetonius	150-225	Acts of Peter and the
115	Tacitus		Twelve
120-130	Quadratus of Athens	150-225	Book of Thomas the
120-130	Apology of Aristides		Contender
120-140	Basilides	150-250	Paraphrase of Shem
120-140	Naassene Fragment	150-250	Fifth and Sixth Books of
120-160	Valentinus		Esra

140

200-300 Coptic Apocalypse of
    Peter
200-330 Apostolic Church Order
200-350 Holy Book of Great
    Invisible Spirit
200-450 Monarchian Prologues
203   Acts of Perpetua and
    Felicitas
203-250 Origen
210-245 Lucian of Antioch
217-222 Callistus
230-265 Dionysius of Alexandria
230-268 Firmilian of Caesarea
240-260 Commodian
246-258 Cyprian
250-274 Gospel of Mani
250-300 Teachings of Silvanus
250-300 Excerpt from the Perfect
    Discourse
250-350 Coptic Apocalypse of
    Elijah
250-400 Apocalypse of Paul
251-253 Pope Cornelius
251-258 Novatian
254-257 Pope Stephen
259-268 Dionysius of Rome
260-280 Theognostus
265-282 Gregory Thaumaturgus
269-274 Pope Felix
270-310 Victorinus of Pettau
270-312 Methodius
270-330 Marsanes
270-330 On the Origin of the
    World
270-350 De Recta in Deum Fide
280-300 Hesychius
280-310 Pierius
280-310 Pamphilus of Caesarea
297-310 Arnobius of Sicca
300-311 Peter of Alexandria
300-320 Pseudo-Clementine
    Homilies
300-340 Eusebius of Caesarea
300-350 Manichean Acts of
    Leucius Charinus

300-390 Letters of Paul and
    Seneca
300-400 Apocalypse of Thomas
300-400 Freer Logion
300-600 Gospel of Gamaliel
303-316 Lactantius
310-334 Reticius of Autun
320-380 Pseudo-Clementine
    Recognitions

Appendix D
ON THE PASCHA

The Peri Pascha of Melito (ca. AD 160-170)

Translation from *Kerux: A Journal of Biblical Theology*, published May 1989.

INTRODUCTION (1-10)

[1] First of all, the Scripture about the Hebrew Exodus has been read and the words of the mystery have been explained as to how the sheep was sacrificed and the people were saved. [2] Therefore, understand this, O beloved: The mystery of the Passover is new and old, eternal and temporal, corruptible and incorruptible, mortal and immortal in this fashion: [3] It is old insofar as it concerns the law, but new insofar as it concerns the gospel; temporal insofar as it concerns the type, eternal because of grace; corruptible because of the sacrifice of the sheep, incorruptible because of the life of the Lord; mortal because of his burial in the earth, immortal because of his resurrection from the dead. [4] The law is old, but the gospel is new; the type was for a time, but grace is forever. The sheep was corruptible, but the Lord is incorruptible, who was crushed as a lamb, but who was resurrected as God. For although he was led to sacrifice as a sheep, yet he was not a sheep; and although he was as a lamb without voice, yet indeed he was not a lamb. The one was the model; the other was found to be the finished product. [5] For God replaced the lamb, and a man the sheep; but in the man was Christ, who contains all things. [6] Hence, the sacrifice of the sheep, and the sending of the lamb to slaughter, and the writing of the law–each led to and issued in Christ, for whose sake everything happened in the ancient law, and even more so in the new gospel. [7] For indeed the law issued in the gospel–the old in the new,

both coming forth together from Zion and Jerusalem; and the commandment issued in grace, and the type in the finished product, and the lamb in the Son, and the sheep in a man, and the man in God. [8] For the one who was born as Son, and led to slaughter as a lamb, and sacrificed as a sheep, and buried as a man, rose up from the dead as God, since he is by nature both God and man. [9] He is everything: in that he judges he is law, in that he teaches he is gospel, in that he saves he is grace, in that he begets he is Father, in that he is begotten he is Son, in that he suffers he is sheep, in that he is buried he is man, in that he comes to life again he is God. [10] Such is Jesus Christ, to whom be the glory forever. Amen.

I. THE MEANING OF THE OT PASSOVER (11-71)

A. The Biblical Setting—Exodus 12:11-30 (11-15)

[11] Now comes the mystery of the Passover, even as it stands written in the law, just as it has been read aloud only moments ago. But I will clearly set forth the significance of the words of this Scripture, showing how God commanded Moses in Egypt, when he had made his decision, to bind Pharaoh under the lash, but to release Israel from the lash through the hand of Moses. [12] For see to it, he says, that you take a flawless and perfect lamb, and that you sacrifice it in the evening with the sons of Israel, and that you eat it at night, and in haste. You are not to break any of its bones. [13] You will do it like this, he says: In a single night you will eat it by families and by tribes, your loins girded, and your staves in your hands. For this is the Lord's Passover, an eternal reminder for the sons of Israel. [14] Then take the blood of the sheep, and anoint the front door of your houses by placing upon the posts of your entrance-way the sign of the blood, in order to ward off the angel. For behold I will strike Egypt, and in a single night she will be made childless from beast to man. [15] Then, when Moses sacrificed the sheep and completed the mystery at night together with the sons of Israel, he

sealed the doors of their houses in order to protect the people and to ward off the angel.

B. Egypt's Calamities (16-29)

[16] But when the sheep was sacrificed, and the Passover consumed, and the mystery completed, and the people made glad, and Israel sealed, then the angel arrived to strike Egypt, who was neither initiated into the mystery, participant of the Passover, sealed by the blood, nor protected by the Spirit, but who was the enemy and the unbeliever. [17] In a single night the angel struck and made Egypt childless. For when the angel had encompassed Israel, and had seen her sealed with the blood of the sheep, he advanced against Egypt, and by means of grief subdued the stubborn Pharaoh, clothing him, not with a cloak of mourning, nor with a torn mantle, but with all of Egypt, torn, and mourning for her firstborn. [18] For all Egypt, plunged in troubles and calamities, in tears and lamentations, came to Pharaoh in utter sadness, not in appearance only, but also in soul, having torn not only her garments but her tender breasts as well. [19] Indeed it was possible to observe an extraordinary sight: in one place people beating their breasts, in another those wailing, and in the middle of them Pharaoh, mourning, sitting in sackcloth and cinders, shrouded in thick darkness as in a funeral garment, girded with all Egypt as with a tunic of grief. [20] For Egypt clothed Pharaoh as a cloak of wailing. Such was the mantle that had been woven for his royal body. With just such a cloak did the angel of righteousness clothe the self-willed Pharaoh: with bitter mournfulness, and with thick darkness, and with childlessness. For that angel warred against the firstborn of Egypt. Indeed, swift and insatiate was the death of the firstborn. [21] And an unusual monument of defeat, set up over those who had fallen dead in a moment, could be seen. For the defeat of those who lay dead became the provisions of death. [22] If you listen to the narration of this extraordinary event you will be astonished. For these things befell the Egyptians: a long night,

and darkness which was touchable, and death which touched, and an angel who oppressed, and Hades which devoured their firstborn.

23 But you must listen to something still more extraordinary and terrifying: in the darkness which could be touched was hidden death which could not be touched. And the ill-starred Egyptians touched the darkness, while death, on the watch, touched the firstborn of the Egyptians as the angel had commanded. 24 Therefore, if anyone touched the darkness he was led out by death. Indeed, one firstborn, touching a dark body with his hand, and utterly frightened in his soul, cried aloud in misery and in terror: What has my right hand laid hold of? At what does my soul tremble? Who cloaks my whole body with darkness? If you are my father, help me; if my mother, feel sympathy for me; if my brother, speak to me; if my friend, sit with me; if my enemy, go away from me since I am a firstborn son! 25 And before the firstborn was silent, the long silence held him in its power, saying: You are mine, O firstborn! I, the silence of death, am your destiny. 26 And another firstborn, taking note of the capture of the firstborn, denied his identity, so that he might not die a bitter death: I am not a firstborn son; I was born like a third child. But he who could not be deceived touched that firstborn, and he fell forward in silence. In a single moment the firstborn fruit of the Egyptians was destroyed. The one first conceived, the one first born, the one sought after, the one chosen was dashed to the ground; not only that of men but that of irrational animals as well. 27 A lowing was heard in the fields of the earth, of cattle bellowing for their nurslings, a cow standing over her calf, and a mare over her colt. And the rest of the cattle, having just given birth to their offspring and swollen with milk, were lamenting bitterly and piteously for their firstborn. 28 And there was a wailing and lamentation because of the destruction of the men, because of the destruction of the firstborn who were dead. And all Egypt stank, because of the unburied bodies. 29 Indeed one could see a frightful spectacle: of the Egyptians there were mothers with disheveled hair, and fathers who had lost their minds,

wailing aloud in terrifying fashion in the Egyptian tongue: O wretched persons that we are! We have lost our firstborn in a single moment! And they were striking their breasts with their hands, beating time in hammerlike fashion to the dance for their dead.

C. Israel's Safety (30-33)

[30] Such was the misfortune which encompassed Egypt. In an instant it made her childless. But Israel, all the while, was being protected by the sacrifice of the sheep and truly was being illumined by its blood which was shed; for the death of the sheep was found to be a rampart for the people. [31] O inexpressible mystery! the sacrifice of the sheep was found to be the salvation of the people, and the death of the sheep became the life of the people. For its blood warded off the angel. [32] Tell me, O angel, At what were you turned away? At the sacrifice of the sheep, or the life of the Lord? At the death of the sheep, or the type of the Lord? At the blood of the sheep, or the Spirit of the Lord? Clearly, you were turned away [33] because you saw the mystery of the Lord taking place in the sheep, the life of the Lord in the sacrifice of the sheep, the type of the Lord in the death of the sheep. For this reason, you did not strike Israel, but it was Egypt alone that you made childless.

D. Model Versus Finished Product (34-38)

[34] What was this extraordinary mystery? It was Egypt struck to destruction but Israel kept for salvation. Listen to the meaning of this mystery: [35] Beloved, no speech or event takes place without a pattern or design; every event and speech involves a pattern–that which is spoken, a pattern, and that which happens, a prefiguration–in order that as the event is disclosed through the prefiguration, so also the speech may be brought to expression through its outline. [36] Without the model, no work of art arises. Is not that which is to come into existence seen through the model which typifies it? For this reason a pattern of that which is to be is made either out of wax, or out of clay, or out of wood,

in order that by the smallness of the model, destined to be destroyed, might be seen that thing which is to arise from it–higher than it in size, and mightier than it in power, and more beautiful than it in appearance, and more elaborate than it in ornamentation. [37] So whenever the thing arises for which the model was made, then that which carried the image of that future thing is destroyed as no longer of use, since it has transmitted its resemblance to that which is by nature true. Therefore, that which once was valuable, is now without value because that which is truly valuable has appeared. [38] For each thing has its own time: there is a distinct time for the type, there is a distinct time for the material, and there is a distinct time for the truth. You construct the model. You want this, because you see in it the image of the future work. You procure the material for the model. You want this, on account of that which is going to arise because of it. You complete the work and cherish it alone, for only in it do you see both type and the truth.

E. Relationship Between OT and NT (39-45)

[39] Therefore, if it was like this with models of perishable objects, so indeed will it also be with those of imperishable objects. If it was like this with earthly things, so indeed also will it be with heavenly things. For even the Lord's salvation and his truth were prefigured in the people, and the teaching of the gospel was proclaimed in advance by the law. [40] The people, therefore, became the model for the church, and the law a parabolic sketch. But the gospel became the explanation of the law and its fulfillment, while the church became the storehouse of truth. [41] Therefore, the type had value prior to its realization, and the parable was wonderful prior to its interpretation. This is to say that the people had value before the church came on the scene, and the law was wonderful before the gospel was brought to light. [42] But when the church came on the scene, and the gospel was set forth, the type lost its value by surrendering its significance to the truth, and the law was fulfilled by surrendering its significance to the gospel. Just as the type

lost its significance by surrendering its image to that which is true by nature, and as the parable lost its significance by being illumined through the interpretation, [43] so indeed also the law was fulfilled when the gospel was brought to light, and the people lost their significance when the church came on the scene, and the type was destroyed when the Lord appeared.

Therefore, those things which once had value are today without value, because the things which have true value have appeared. [44] For at one time the sacrifice to the sheep was valuable, but now it is without value because of the life of the Lord. The death of the sheep once was valuable, but now it is without value because of the salvation of the Lord. The blood of the sheep once was valuable, but now it is without value because of the Spirit of the Lord. The silent lamb once was valuable, but now it has no value because of the blameless Son. The temple here below once was valuable, but now it is without value because of the Christ from above. [45] The Jerusalem here below once had value, but now it is without value because of the Jerusalem from above. The meager inheritance once had value; now it is without value because of the abundant grace. For not in one place alone, nor yet in narrow confines, has the glory of God been established, but his grace has been poured out upon the uttermost parts of the inhabited world, and there the almighty God has taken up his dwelling place through Jesus Christ, to whom be the glory for ever. Amen.

F. Components of the Mystery of the Passover (46-71)

1. The Passover (46-47a)

[46] Now that you have heard the explanation of the type and of that which corresponds to it, hear also what goes into making up the mystery. What is the Passover? Indeed its name is derived from that event–"to celebrate the Passover" (to paschein) is derived from "to suffer" (tou pathein). Therefore, learn who the sufferer is and who he

is who suffers along with the sufferer. [47a] Why indeed was the Lord present upon the earth? In order that having clothed himself with the one who suffers, he might lift him up to the heights of heaven.

2. The Creation and Fall of Man (47b-48)

[47b] In the beginning, when God made heaven and earth, and everything in them through his word, he himself formed man from the earth and shared with that form his own breath, he himself placed him in paradise, which was eastward in Eden, and there they lived most luxuriously. Then by way of command God gave them this law: For your food you may eat from any tree, but you are not to eat from the tree of the one who knows good and evil. For on the day you eat from it, you most certainly will die. [48] But man, who is by nature capable of receiving good and evil as soil of the earth is capable of receiving seeds from both sides, welcomed the hostile and greedy counselor, and by having touched that tree transgressed the command, and disobeyed God. As a consequence, he was cast out into this world as a condemned man is cast into prison.

3. Consequences of the Fall (49-56)

[49] And when he had fathered many children, and had grown very old, and had returned to the earth through having tasted of the tree, an inheritance was left behind by him for his children. Indeed, he left his children an inheritance–not of chastity but of unchastity, not of immortality but of corruptibility, not of honor but of dishonor, not of freedom but of slavery, not of sovereignty but of tyranny, not of life but of death, not of salvation but of destruction. [50] Extraordinary and terrifying indeed was the destruction of men upon the earth. For the following things happened to them: They were carried off as slaves by sin, the tyrant, and were led away into the regions of desire where they were totally engulfed by insatiable sensual pleasures–by adultery, by unchastity, by debauchery, by inordinate desires, by avarice, by

murders, by bloodshed, by the tyranny of wickedness, by the tyranny of lawlessness. [51] For even a father of his own accord lifted up a dagger against his son; and a son used his hands against his father; and the impious person smote the breasts that nourished him; and brother murdered brother; and host wronged his guest; and friend assassinated friend; and one man cut the throat of another with his tyrannous right hand.

[52] Therefore all men on the earth became either murderers, or parricides, or killers of their children. And yet a thing still more dreadful and extraordinary was to be found: A mother attacked the flesh which she gave birth to, a mother attacked those whom her breasts had nourished; and she buried in her belly the fruit of her belly. Indeed, the ill-starred mother became a dreadful tomb, when she devoured the child which she bore in her womb. [53] But in addition to this there were to be found among men many things still more monstrous and terrifying and brutal: father cohabits with his child, and son and with his mother, and brother with sister, and male with male, and each man lusting after the wife of his neighbor. [54] Because of these things sin exulted, which, because it was death's collaborator, entered first into the souls of men, and prepared as food for him the bodies of the dead. In every soul sin left its mark, and those in whom it placed its mark were destined to die. [55] Therefore, all flesh fell under the power of sin, and every body under the dominion of death, for every soul was driven out from its house of flesh. Indeed, that which had been taken from the earth was dissolved again into earth, and that which had been given from God was locked up in Hades. And that beautiful ordered arrangement was dissolved, when the beautiful body was separated (from the soul). [56] Yes, man was divided up into parts by death. Yes, an extraordinary misfortune and captivity enveloped him: he was dragged away captive under the shadow of death, and the image of the Father remained there desolate. For this reason, therefore,

the mystery of the Passover has been completed in the body of the Lord.

4. Predictions of Christ's Sufferings (57-65)

[57] Indeed, the Lord prearranged his own sufferings in the patriarchs, and in the prophets, and in the whole people of God, giving his sanction to them through the law and the prophets. For that which was to exist in a new and grandiose fashion was pre-planned long in advance, in order that when it should come into existence one might attain to faith, just because it had been predicted long in advance. [58] So indeed also the suffering of the Lord, predicted long in advance by means of types, but seen today, has brought about faith, just because it has taken place as predicted. And yet men have taken it as something completely new. Well, the truth of the matter is the mystery of the Lord is both old and new—old insofar as it involved the type, but new insofar as it concerns grace. And what is more, if you pay close attention to this type you will see the real thing through its fulfillment. [59] Accordingly, if you desire to see the mystery of the Lord, pay close attention to Abel who likewise was put to death, to Isaac who likewise was bound hand and foot, to Joseph who likewise was sold, to Moses who likewise was exposed, to David who likewise was hunted down, to the prophets who likewise suffered because they were the Lord's anointed. [60] Pay close attention also to the one who was sacrificed as a sheep in the land of Egypt, to the one who smote Egypt and who saved Israel by his blood. [61] For it was through the voice of prophecy that the mystery of the Lord was proclaimed. Moses, indeed, said to his people: Surely you will see your life suspended before your eyes night and day, but you surely will not believe on your Life (Deut. 28:66). [62] And David said: Why were the nations haughty and the people concerned about nothing? The kings of the earth presented themselves and the princes assembled themselves together against the Lord and against his anointed (Ps. 2:1-2). [63] And Jeremiah: I am as an innocent lamb being led away to be

sacrificed. They plotted evil against me and said: Come! let us throw him a tree for his food, and let us exterminate him from the land of the living, so that his name will never be recalled (Jer. 11:19). [64] And Isaiah: He was led as a sheep to slaughter, and, as a lamb is silent in the presence of the one who shears it, he did not open his mouth. Therefore, who will tell his offspring? (Isa. 53:7) [65] And indeed there were many other things proclaimed by numerous prophets concerning the mystery of the passover, which is Christ, to whom be the glory forever. Amen.

5. Deliverance of Mankind through Christ (66-71)

[66] When this one came from heaven to earth for the sake of the one who suffers, and had clothed himself with that very one through the womb of a virgin, and having come forth as man, he accepted the sufferings of the sufferer through his body which was capable of suffering. And he destroyed those human sufferings by his spirit which was incapable of dying. He killed death which had put man to death. [67] For this one, who was led away as a lamb, and who was sacrificed as a sheep, by himself delivered us from servitude to the world as from the land of Egypt, and released us from bondage to the devil as from the hand of Pharaoh, and sealed our souls by his own spirit and the members of our bodies by his own blood. [68] This is the one who covered death with shame and who plunged the devil into mourning as Moses did Pharaoh. This is the one who smote lawlessness and deprived injustice of its offspring, as Moses deprived Egypt. This is the one who delivered us from slavery into freedom, from darkness into light, from death into life, from tyranny into an eternal kingdom, and who made us a new priesthood, and a special people forever. [69] This one is the Passover of our salvation. This is the one who patiently endured many things in many people: This is the one who was murdered in Abel, and bound as a sacrifice in Isaac, and exiled in Jacob, and sold in Joseph, and exposed in Moses, and sacrificed in the

lamb, and hunted down in David, and dishonored in the prophets. [70] This is the one who became human in a virgin, who was hanged on the tree, who was buried in the earth, who was resurrected from among the dead, and who raised mankind up out of the grave below to the heights of heaven. [71] This is the lamb that was slain. This is the lamb that was silent. This is the one who was born of Mary, that beautiful ewe-lamb. This is the one who was taken from the flock, and was dragged to sacrifice, and was killed in the evening, and was buried at night; the one who was not broken while on the tree, who did not see dissolution while in the earth, who rose up from the dead, and who raised up mankind from the grave below.

II. THE DEATH OF CHRIST AND ISRAEL'S SIN (72-99)

A. Place and Cause of Christ's Death (72-86)

[72] This one was murdered. And where was he murdered? In the very center of Jerusalem! Why? Because he had healed their lame, and had cleansed their lepers, and had guided their blind with light, and had raised up their dead. For this reason, he suffered. Somewhere it has been written in the law and prophets, "They paid me back evil for good, and my soul with barrenness (Ps. 34:12) plotting evil against me (Ps. 34:4; 40:8) saying, Let us bind this just man because he is troublesome to us" (Isa. 3:10 (LXX)). [73] Why, O Israel did you do this strange injustice? You dishonored the one who had honored you. You held in contempt the one who held you in esteem. You denied the one who publicly acknowledged you. You renounced the one who proclaimed you his own. You killed the one who made you to live. Why did you do this, O Israel? [74] Hast it not been written for your benefit: "Do not shed innocent blood lest you die a terrible death"? Nevertheless, Israel admits, I killed the Lord! Why? Because it was necessary for him to die. You have deceived yourself, O Israel, rationalizing thus about the

death of the Lord. [75] It was necessary for him to suffer, yes, but not by you; it was necessary for him to be dishonored, but not by you; it was necessary for him to be judged, but not by you; it was necessary for him to be crucified, but not by you, nor by your right hand. [76] O Israel! You ought to have cried aloud to God with this voice: "O Lord, if it was necessary for your Son to suffer, and if this was your will, let him suffer indeed, but not at my hands. Let him suffer at the hands of strangers. Let him be judged by the uncircumcised. Let him be crucified by the tyrannical right hand, but not by mine." [77] But you, O Israel, did not cry out to God with this voice, nor did you absolve yourself of guilt before the Lord, nor were you persuaded by his works. [78] The withered hand which was restored whole to its body did not persuade you; nor did the eyes of the blind which were opened by his hand; nor did the paralyzed bodies restored to health again through his voice; nor did that most extraordinary miracle persuade you, namely, the dead man raised to life from the tomb where already he had been lying for four days. Indeed, dismissing these things, you, to your detriment, prepared the following for the sacrifice of the Lord at eventide: sharp nails, and false witnesses, and fetters, and scourges, [79] and vinegar, and gall, and a sword, and affliction, and all as though it were for a blood-stained robber. For you brought to him scourges for his body, and the thorns for his head. And you bound those beautiful hands of his, which had formed you from the earth. And that beautiful mouth of his, which had nourished you with life, you filled with gall. And you killed your Lord at the time of the great feast. [80] Surely you were filled with gaiety, but he was filled with hunger; you drank wine and ate bread, but he vinegar and gall; you wore a happy smile, but he had a sad countenance; you were full of joy, but he was full of trouble; you sang songs, but he was judged; you issued the command, he was crucified; you danced, he was buried; you lay down on a soft bed, but he in a tomb and coffin.

[81] O lawless Israel, why did you commit this extraordinary crime of casting your Lord into new sufferings–your master, the one who formed you, the one who made you, the one who honored you, the one who called you Israel? [82] But you were found not really to be Israel, for you did not see God, you did not recognize the Lord, you did not know, O Israel, that this one was the firstborn of God, the one who was begotten before the morning star, the one who caused the light to shine forth, the one who made bright the day, the one who parted the darkness, the one who established the primordial starting point, the one who suspended the earth, the one who quenched the abyss, the one who stretched out the firmament, the one who formed the universe, [83] the one who set in motion the stars of heaven, the one who caused those luminaries to shine, the one who made the angels in heaven, the one who established their thrones in that place, the one who by himself fashioned man upon the earth. This was the one who chose you, the one who guided you from Adam to Noah, from Noah to Abraham, from Abraham to Isaac and Jacob and the Twelve Patriarchs. [84] This was the one who guided you into Egypt, and guarded you, and himself kept you well supplied there. This was the one who lighted your route with a column of fire, and provided shade for you by means of a cloud, the one who divided the Red Sea, and led you across it, and scattered your enemy abroad. [85] This is the one who provided you with manna from heaven, the one who gave you water to drink from a rock, the one who established your laws in Horeb, the one who gave you an inheritance in the land, the one who sent out his prophets to you, the one who raised up your kings. [86] This is the one who came to you, the one who healed your suffering ones and who resurrected your dead. This is the one whom you sinned against. This is the one whom you wronged. This is the one whom you killed. This is the one whom you sold for silver, although you asked him for the didrachma.

B. Israel Brought to Trial (87-93)

[87] O ungrateful Israel, come here and be judged before me for your ingratitude. How high a price did you place on being created by him? How high a price did you place on the discovery of your fathers? How high a price did you place on the descent into Egypt, and the provision made for you there through the noble Joseph? [88] How high a price did you place on the ten plagues? How high a price did you place on the nightly column of fire, and the daily cloud, and the crossing of the Red Sea? How high a price did you place on the gift of manna from heaven, and the gift of water from the rock, and the gift of law in Horeb, and the land as an inheritance, and the benefits accorded you there? [89] How high a price did you place on your suffering people whom he healed when he was present? Set me a price on the withered hand, which he restored whole to its body. [90] Put me a price on the men born blind, whom he led into light by his voice. Put me a price on those who lay dead, whom he raised up alive from the tomb. Inestimable are the benefits that come to you from him. But you, shamefully, have paid him back with ingratitude, returning to him evil for good, and affliction for favor and death for life—[91] a person for whom you should have died. Furthermore, if the king of some nation is captured by an enemy, a war is started because of him, fortifications are shattered because of him, cities are plundered because of him, ransom is sent because of him, ambassadors are commissioned because of him in order that he might be surrendered, so that either he might be returned if living, or that he might be buried if dead.

[92] But you, quite to the contrary, voted against your Lord, whom indeed the nations worshipped, and the uncircumcised admired, and the foreigners glorified, over whom Pilate washed his hands. But as for you—you killed this one at the time of the great feast. [93] Therefore, the feast of unleavened bread has become bitter to you just as it was written: "You will eat unleavened bread with bitter herbs." Bitter to you are the nails which you made pointed. Bitter to you is the tongue

which you sharpened. Bitter to you are the false witnesses whom you brought forward. Bitter to you are the fetters which you prepared. Bitter to you are the scourges which you wove. Bitter to you is Judas whom you furnished with pay. Bitter to you is Herod whom you followed. Bitter to you is Caiaphas whom you obeyed. Bitter to you is the gall which you made ready. Bitter to you is the vinegar which you produced. Bitter to you are the thorns which you plucked. Bitter to you are your hands which you bloodied, when you killed your Lord in the midst of Jerusalem.

C. Gentiles Are Witnesses of Israel's Crime (94-98)

[94] Pay attention, all families of the nations, and observe! An extraordinary murder has taken place in the center of Jerusalem, in the city devoted to God's law, in the city of the Hebrews, in the city of the prophets, in the city thought of as just. And who has been murdered? And who is the murderer? I am ashamed to give the answer, but give it I must. For if this murder had taken place at night, or if he had been slain in a desert place, it would be well to keep silent; but it was in the middle of the main street, even in the center of the city, while all were looking on, that the unjust murder of this just person took place. [95] And thus he was lifted up upon the tree, and an inscription was affixed identifying the one who had been murdered. Who was he? It is painful to tell, but it is more dreadful not to tell. Therefore, hear and tremble because of him for whom the earth trembled.

[96] The one who hung the earth in space, is himself hanged; the one who fixed the heavens in place, is himself impaled; the one who firmly fixed all things, is himself firmly fixed to the tree. The Lord is insulted, God has been murdered, the King of Israel has been destroyed by the right hand of Israel. [97] O frightful murder! O unheard of injustice! The Lord is disfigured and he is not deemed worthy of a cloak for his naked body, so that he might not be seen exposed. For this reason the stars turned and fled, and the day grew quite dark, in order to hide the naked

person hanging on the tree, darkening not the body of the Lord, but the eyes of men. [98] Yes, even though the people did not tremble, the earth trembled instead; although the people were not afraid, the heavens grew frightened; although the people did not tear their garments, the angels tore theirs; although the people did not lament, the Lord thundered from heaven, and the most high uttered his voice.

D. Israel Questioned and Sentenced to Death (99)

[99] Why was it like this, O Israel? You did not tremble for the Lord. You did not fear for the Lord. You did not lament for the Lord, yet you lamented for your firstborn. You did not tear your garments at the crucifixion of the Lord, yet you tore your garments for your own who were murdered. You forsook the Lord; you were not found by him. You dashed the Lord to the ground; you, too, were dashed to the ground, and lie quite dead.

III. THE FINAL TRIUMPH OF CHRIST (100-105)

[100] But he arose from the dead and mounted up to the heights of heaven. When the Lord had clothed himself with humanity, and had suffered for the sake of the sufferer, and had been bound for the sake of the imprisoned, and had been judged for the sake of the condemned, and buried for the sake of the one who was buried, [101] he rose up from the dead, and cried aloud with this voice: Who is he who contends with me? Let him stand in opposition to me. I set the condemned man free; I gave the dead man life; I raised up the one who had been entombed. [102] Who is my opponent? I, he says, am the Christ. I am the one who destroyed death, and triumphed over the enemy, and trampled Hades under foot, and bound the strong one, and carried off man to the heights of heaven, I, he says, am the Christ.

[103] Therefore, come, all families of men, you who have been befouled with sins, and receive forgiveness for your sins. I am your forgiveness, I am the Passover of your salvation, I am the lamb which

was sacrificed for you, I am your ransom, I am your light, I am your savior, I am your resurrection, I am your king, I am leading you up to the heights of heaven, I will show you the eternal Father, I will raise you up by my right hand. [104] This is the one who made the heavens and the earth, and who in the beginning created man, who was proclaimed through the law and prophets, who became human via the virgin, who was hanged upon a tree, who was buried in the earth, who was resurrected from the dead, and who ascended to the heights of heaven, who sits at the right hand of the Father, who has authority to judge and to save everything, through whom the Father created everything from the beginning of the world to the end of the age. [105] This is the alpha and the omega. This is the beginning and the end–an indescribable beginning and an incomprehensible end. This is the Christ. This is the king. This is Jesus. This is the general. This is the Lord. This is the one who rose up from the dead. This is the one who sits at the right hand of the Father. He bears the Father and is borne by the Father, to whom be the glory and the power forever. Amen.

Appendix E

ON THE KEEPING OF EASTER

(Found in Eusebius, *Vita Const.,* Lib. iii., 18–20.)

From the Letter of the Emperor to all those not present at the Council:

When the question relative to the sacred festival of Easter arose, it was universally thought that it would be convenient that all should keep the feast on one day; for what could be more beautiful and more desirable, than to see this festival, through which we receive the hope of immortality, celebrated by all with one accord, and in the same manner? It was declared to be particularly unworthy for this, the holiest of all festivals, to follow the custom [the calculation] of the Jews, who had soiled their hands with the most fearful of crimes, and whose minds were blinded. In rejecting their custom, we may transmit to our descendants the legitimate mode of celebrating Easter, which we have observed from the time of the Savior's Passion to the present day [according to the day of the week]. We ought not, therefore, to have anything in common with the Jews, for the Savior has shown us another way; our worship follows a more legitimate and more convenient course (the order of the days of the week); and consequently, in unanimously adopting this mode, we desire, dearest brethren, to separate ourselves from the detestable company of the Jews, for it is truly shameful for us to hear them boast that without their direction we could not keep this feast. How can they be in the right, they who, after the death of the Savior, have no longer been led by reason but by wild violence, as their delusion may urge them? They do not possess the truth in this Easter question; for, in their blindness and repugnance to all improvements, they frequently celebrate two passovers in the same year. We could not imitate those who are openly in error. How, then, could we follow these Jews, who are most certainly blinded by error? for to celebrate the passover twice in one year is totally inadmissible. But even if this were not so, it would still be your duty not to tarnish your soul by communications with such wicked people [the Jews]. Besides, consider well, that in such an important matter, and on a subject of such great solemnity, there ought not to be any division. Our Savior has left us only one festal day of our redemption, that is to say, of his holy passion, and he desired [to establish] only one Catholic Church. Think, then, how unseemly it is, that on the same day some should be fasting whilst others are seated at a banquet; and that after Easter, some should be rejoicing at feasts, whilst others are still observing a strict fast. For this reason, a Divine Providence wills that this custom should be rectified and regulated in a uniform way; and everyone, I hope, will agree upon this point. As, on the one hand, it is our duty not to have anything in common with the murderers of our Lord; and as, on the other, the custom now followed by the Churches of the West, of the South, and of the North, and by some of those of the East, is the most acceptable, it has appeared good to all; and I have been guarantee for your consent, that you would accept it with joy, as it is followed at Rome, in Africa, in all Italy, Egypt, Spain, Gaul, Britain, Libya, in all Achaia, and in the dioceses of Asia, of Pontus, and Cilicia. You should consider not only that the number of churches in these provinces make a majority, but also that it is right to demand what our reason approves, and that we should have nothing in common with the Jews.

To sum up in few words: By the unanimous judgment of all, it has been decided that the most holy festival of Easter should be everywhere celebrated on one and the same day, and it is not seemly that in so holy a thing there should be any division. As this is the state of the case, accept joyfully the divine favor, and this truly divine command; for all which takes place in assemblies of the bishops ought to be regarded as proceeding from the will of God. Make known to your brethren what has been decreed, keep this most holy day according to the prescribed mode; we can thus celebrate this holy Easter day at the same time, if it is granted me, as I desire, to unite myself with you; we can rejoice together, seeing that the divine power has made use of our instrumentality for destroying the evil designs of the devil, and thus causing faith, peace, and unity to flourish amongst us.

May God graciously protect you, my beloved brethren.

Made in the USA
Columbia, SC
04 July 2021